Everyone Needs Jesus

The Meat of the Word for Christians Today Volume 2

Everyone Needs Jesus

by
Pastor Willie F. Pride, Jr.

Everlasting Publishing
Yakima, Washington
USA

Everyone Needs Jesus

Volume 2 of
The Meat of the Word for Christians Today

by
Pastor Willie F. Pride, Jr.

ISBN: 0-9824844-3-7
ISBN 13: 978-0-9824844-3-2

First Edition
Everlasting Publishing
P.O. Box 1061
Yakima, WA 98907
USA

Truly, we thank God for His Word,
for heaven and earth will pass away,
but God's Word will stand forever.

Dedicated to

Everyone who loves Jesus

and

Everyone who needs Jesus

Contents

BINDING TOGETHER IN THE NAME OF JESUS
Matthew 16:18-19, II Timothy 4:2-5

We're thankful to the Lord today for each of you, for the Bible tells us that faith cometh by hearing, and hearing by the Word of God. How can you hear without a preacher, and how can they preach, unless they be sent? Truly we're thankful to God today for your prayers, and we're thankful to the Lord for His Word. For the Bible says where two or three are assembled and gathered together in His name, that He would be a God in the midst. Truly we thank God today for being in the midst of us right now.

We're thankful to the Lord today that we are a light, and a light shining upon a hill that should be seen. Would you turn with me this morning to just a couple of books today? St. Matthew, chapter 16, if you would turn with me to that, and along with that, would you turn with me to Second Timothy, chapter 4 also. St. Matthew, chapter 16, II Timothy, chapter 4. How many of you have your Bibles? Praise the Lord. We're thankful to the Lord for our visitors today. We know that God knows and cares about us and about situations that are happening in our world today.

St. Matthew, chapter 16, verses 18-19, where our reading is coming from.

18. And I say also unto thee, That thou art Peter, and upon this rock I will build my church; and the gates of hell shall not prevail against it.
19. And I will give unto thee the keys of the kingdom of heaven: and whatsoever thou shalt bind on earth shall be bound in heaven: and whatsoever thou shalt loose on earth shall be loosed in heaven.

Let us turn now to II Timothy, the 4th chapter, verses 2-5.

2. Preach the word; be instant in season, out of season; reprove, rebuke, exhort with all long suffering and doctrine.
3. For the time will come when they will not endure sound doctrine; but after their own lusts shall they heap to themselves teachers, having itching ears;

4. And they shall turn away their ears from the truth, and shall be turned unto fables.

5. But watch thou in all things, endure afflictions, do the work of an evangelist, make full proof of thy ministry.

I want to talk about a thought or a subject today, if you will, that you might carry home with you today, "Binding Together in the Name of Jesus." Would you say that with me? "Binding Together in the Name of Jesus."

A few months ago, a dear sister and I were praying about some situations, and as we prayed, it didn't seem that things were happening as we felt that they should have been happening. We prayed all the more, and one specific afternoon, she and I had been praying, and she was pretty much frustrated because God hadn't moved as fast as she thought He should have been moving. I said to her, "Sister, let's apply the Word. We've applied our strength and nothing's happened. We've applied the law, and nothing's happened. We've applied all of the intellect that we could possibly muster, and nothing's happened. We have applied everything that we could think of, and nothing has happened." But then the Spirit of God dealt with me on that particular afternoon, and said that when you bind together, and whatever you bind together on earth shall be bound together in heaven, as touching and agreeing on the same thing. I said that to someone prior to this situation, and they said to me, "That doesn't mean that. It doesn't mean that you're binding together. It simply means something else." And I said, "I don't know what it means. I just know we need to bind together, believing that heaven is binding together, and Jesus said, 'whatever you bind on earth shall be bound in heaven, as touching and agreeing on the same thing.' " Do you not know that some situations in our lives, we need to get with somebody, we need to agree together, according to God's Word and His will. My sister and I touched and agreed. Do you not know that when we touched and agreed, we saw God move right then! We saw God begin to take control of situations and begin to move in a mighty way. Not that our will was being done, but that God's will was being done. You ought to hear me today.

We're thankful to the Lord today for binding together in the name of Jesus. Let us pray.

Our Father, we thank You now for what You've done and are going to do. Oh, heavenly Father, we need You right now. Oh, heavenly Father, You said if You be lifted up, You would draw all men. We want to lift You up today. Oh, heavenly Father, use these lips of clay, not my will, but let Thy will be done. Open up our blind eyes today. Open up deaf ears today, in the name of Jesus. Oh, Lord God, we're standing on Your Word. We're standing on Your promises. Lord God, we need You right now. We're asking You to continue to lend us your Spirit today, in the name of Jesus. Pour out upon us today, in the name of Jesus. Lord God, faith cometh by hearing, and hearing by the Word of God. We need, Lord God, more faith today. We need the power of Your Word today, for much prayer, much power; little prayer, little power; no prayer, no power. We want much prayer today, in the name of Jesus. Now, Lord, use me in a mighty way. In Jesus' name we pray, and we give You the glory right now. Amen.

Binding together in the name of Jesus. Jesus says, "And I will give unto thee the keys of the kingdom of heaven, and whatsoever thou shalt bind on earth shall be bound in heaven. And whatsoever thou shalt loose on earth shall be loosed in heaven." "Preach the Word," also, in II Timothy 4:2-4. "Preach the word, and be instant in season and out of season." Oh, my sisters and brothers, it ought to be something about your Christian walk, you ought to be consistent. Oh, I tell folks everywhere I go, you take some of the biggest fools in the world, and they're consistent in being what they are. They are fools consistently. They don't waver. As Christians, we ought to be consistent. We ought to be what we say we are. We say, "I'm going to let my light shine," then our lights ought to shine everywhere we go.

Then we see also in II Timothy 4:2-4, it says, "the time will come that they will not endure sound doctrine, but after their own lusts shall they heap to themselves teachers, having itching ears, and they shall turn away their ears from the truth, and shall be turned unto fables." In the conversation between Jesus and Peter, we find some challenging information as it relates to the preacher's task in advancing the kingdom of God. We see that Paul's saying, "Be instant in season and out of season." We can see after Peter's answer to the most famous question, Jesus was totally satisfied that His Father had sanctioned one of His earthly followers to be the key man, after His mission here was completed. For He said to Peter that it wasn't upon Peter that He built His church, but it was upon the testimony that Peter had given, that Jesus was the Son of God, the Son of the true and living God, the One that came and would take away the sins of the world.

Oh, we see that with divine authority He cannot only commission Peter, but He also gives directions to us. He tells us that we must minister, or preach the Word, in season and out of season. You might say, "Brother Pastor, I can't preach like somebody else can preach. I can't teach like somebody else can teach." But you ought to know within yourself that God has given you something to do. He's given you something to share with the world. He's given you something that maybe nobody else has. But He says to us, binding together, coming together in the name of Jesus, knowing that there's something about that name, knowing there's something about that mighty name. I don't know about you today, but maybe you've never been sick. But I know there's power in that name. There's medicine and healing in that name. Look at the account today of the woman who touched the hem of His garment. She said, "If I could just reach out and touch the hem of His garment, I could be made whole." Oh, I'm glad today, there's power in that name.

There's power when God's people begin to bind together. Look at the day of Pentecost. It says they came together on one accord. They were all on one accord and they were praying that God would move in their situation. I don't know about you today, but whatever it is that you might be going through, you ought to be binding together with the Word of God. You ought to be binding together with the Spirit of God, knowing that whatever you bind on earth shall be bound in heaven, as touching and agreeing on the same thing. Oh, we see this morning, clearly from heaven's authority He gives him the authority to bind and to loose. He said that whatever you bind on earth shall be bound in heaven. To bind, as it relates to Peter's authority, is to put under constraints or obligation with response to what you're asking the Lord to do. What Jesus is really saying to Peter, in layman's language, is this, "Peter, whatever is wrong here on earth, My Father and I are expecting you to correct it." So the preacher, like Peter, God is using him and using you to accomplish the things that God wants you to accomplish.

Jesus, in His statement to Peter, uses another word. He says "loose," and whatsoever you shall loose on earth shall be loosed in heaven, as He says. Well, let us examine this all-important word in the life and duties of a preacher or minister or those who are carrying the cross for Jesus Christ. First of all, it relates to his task, advancing the cause of Christ. A quick decision must be made. Sometimes it affects the best of friends, but as God's messenger, as God's disciple, as one being used by God, you ought to know that God is first in your life, and that He has a promise for each of us, for Paul said that the race is not given to the swiftest, it's not given to the strongest, but to him that endureth to the end.

I don't know about you today, but you ought to be stirring up that Jesus is coming back. Somebody would say to me this morning, "Brother Pastor, do you know when the Lord is coming?" I don't know the day or the hour, but I know He's coming back. And I know that we better not be talking about all of this, "I'm going to get ready." We ought to be ready when He comes.

Oh, I'm glad today, for when we bind together in the name of Jesus, we can begin to see the Spirit of God flow. We can begin to see healings come about. We can begin to see miracles on every hand begin to come about. We can begin to see where the devil is trying to steal your joy, the joy will begin to come about. Oh, I'm glad this morning. I'm glad that God gave you and me something that the world didn't give and the world can't take away. Everywhere you go, you ought to tell somebody, "I know the Lord." I know that He's a doctor in a sick room. I know the Lord, He might have been a lawyer for me, in a courtroom. I know the Lord, He might have been bread when I was hungry.

I don't know about you today, but binding together in the name of Jesus makes the difference. You might say this morning, "Brother Pastor, I'm binding together," but are you binding according to His Word? Are you binding according to what the Lord says? Oh, my sisters and my brothers, He also says, and Paul goes a little further in his letter to Timothy, for he gives him the challenging order and authority, for he says, "rebuke, reprove, and exhort." Men and women now days are not receptive to sound doctrine. To follow through on this astonishing fact of Paul, he's saying to us, be rooted and grounded in the Word. Be rooted and grounded in the Word of God. Oh, I'm glad this morning for the Sunday School lesson, for it was talking about this same situation, where people had heard things. They had heard what others had said, but they weren't doing what the Word says. But Paul straightened them out when he said to them, "I preached no other message than that of Jesus Christ, His death, burial and resurrection, and His coming back again."

I don't know about you today, but you ought to be binding together with the Word of God. You ought to be binding together with the Spirit of God, knowing that it's the only thing that can lead and guide you. It's the only thing that will help you make it through. Oh, I'm glad this morning, that binding together does make a difference. Binding together can change the heart. Binding together can change the mind. Binding together can change the walk. Binding together can do something for you on the inside. Oh, I'm glad today! I'm glad that I'm not following a denomination, but I'm following the Lord and Savior, Jesus Christ. Somebody would say today, "Well, I'm following the preacher." Let me tell you today, you don't want to follow the preacher. You don't want to follow the deacon board. But you want to follow Jesus, the One who sits high and looks low. Binding together in the name of Jesus.

Oh, I'm glad today! I'm glad that God is still pouring out His Spirit! I'm glad, He's still sanctifying, and He's still filling! One must be able to say today, as Peter and Paul, when the turbulent waters of life were about to drown them, Peter was put in jail for preaching Christ. He was telling the Jewish community that "the same Jesus whom you crucified, the third day morning who rose, is coming back to judge every man." The same Jesus, hallelujah! that they hung there on the cross, is coming back again! The same Jesus that died for your sins and my sins, and the sins of the world, is coming back again! Oh, I'm glad today! I'm glad that we're binding together in the name of Jesus. I don't know about you this morning, but you ought to have your hand in God's hands. You ought to have your mind stayed on Him. He's the only One that can turn midnights into day! He's the only One that can create a love - oh, glory to God!

Paul astonished the intellectual community when he said, "Jew and Greek, it doesn't matter with God. God is no respecter of persons." Oh, I'm glad today! I'm glad that Jesus is sitting high! I'm glad today that Jesus is pouring out His Spirit! I'm glad this morning that nobody, nobody can do you like Jesus! Put your hand, Church, in God's hand! Put your hands in the hands of the Man that can still the waters in our times! Oh, this morning, when we get together, things begin to happen! When we get together, God begins to move in a mighty way! I want to say to you today, let the Lord move in your life! Let the Lord fix you up! Let the Lord turn your midnights into day! And He will! He will! He will today, open up the windows of heaven! I'm trying to close here, but it's something about Jesus! You ought to not be the keeper of yourself! You ought to be kept by the power and by the Word of God! You ought to be washed - hallelujah - in the blood of the Lamb! Don't you know there's power? There's power in His name! You can call on Him at noon day! You can call on Him at midnight! You can call on Him and He will turn it around! He will turn your midnights into day!

I'm trying to close here, but it's something about binding together in His name, in the name of Jesus! There's power, wonder-working power, saving power, delivering power, in His name today! Put your hand in the hand of the Man who is able today! Binding together in His name! His name today! There's power, wonder-working power in the blood of the Lamb! The Lamb of God, the One that taketh away the sins of the world! I'm glad this morning that Jesus came down! Oh, glory to God! He came down to this earth, walked the earth for thirty-three and a half years, letting us know that He is real, and we, too, have to walk. But let me tell you today, He was doing the will of His Father! I don't know about you today! You ought to be doing the will, not of your earthly father, but of your heavenly Father! You ought to today, know that God is leading and guiding! I'm glad today! I'm glad for Jesus, the mighty Lamb of God. I'm glad! I'm glad that God so loved the world that He sent His Son, His only begotten Son, down to the world for you and me, that we might have life, and life more abundantly! I'm glad that we don't need a sacrifice any more! We don't need a lamb, and we don't need a dove. We don't need a bullock or any other sacrifice! We don't even need a burnt pig! Oh, bless God's holy name! But Jesus, the mighty Lamb of God, He died! He came down, that we might have life, and life more abundantly! I'm glad that Jesus came down from Calvary, all the way down, oh, glory to God! Just imagine today, some of us, as low-down, dirty sinners as we were, and as some of us are, we'd still be trying to find a sacrifice to wash away our sins. But, Jesus! I can go to Him and tell the Lord, "Lord, I'm sorry, forgive me right now," and He will! As I bind together on His Word, He will, today, forgive me of my sins! He will! He will send the Comforter that will lead you and guide you!

Oh, I'm glad today, I'm not the keeper of myself! I feel something now! I know what it is! It's not me, Lord! I'm out of self now! Oh, bless His holy name! I'm going up a little bit higher! Another round up! I know what it is now, I'm getting on board! One thing about yourself, you ought to know when the Lord lifts you up! I'm lifted up a little bit higher!

Oh, Lord! Oh, Lord, help us today, to bind together in Your name! Help us today, Lord, to stand on Your Word! Help us today, oh, Lord! Oh, Jesus, oh, glory to God! Thank You, Jesus, for what you're doing right now! Thank You, Lord, for sound doctrine today!

It's not the water, it's not the blood, it's Jesus! Oh, bless His name! Jesus! We can stand on Him today! Jesus! Oh, glory! Jesus! Will you say that with me! It ought to be a stirring on the inside! When you say that wonderful name: Jesus! I don't know what your condition is, but when you say "Jesus," something ought to begin to happen. Shackles ought to break! Healings ought to come about! Glory to God! Feelings on the inside that might be hatred ought to begin to turn to love! Oh, Lord, distorted minds ought to go away when you start talking about Jesus!

I guarantee you today, there's power when we bind together! I'm trying to close here! We've got two more services today, but I'm not worried! The Lord said He would let rivers of living water flow out of our bellies! Oh, Lord! Oh, Lord, I'm glad today! He can fill us up! Oh, glory to God! And you will never run dry! You will never dry out! You will never! Oh, glory to God! Thank You, Jesus! Binding together in the name of the Lord. I'm glad today, for sound doctrine this morning! Oh, bless His holy name! Thank You, Lord! And Jesus was hanging there on the cross, blood running down from His hands and His feet, but He didn't say a mumbling word. He looked out over Calvary and said, "Father! Father, forgive them, for they know not what they do!" I'm glad this morning that Jesus set an example, an example for you and me that we all ought to follow! He didn't say, "I'm going to call a legion of angels and I'm going to destroy the world," but He said, "Forgive them, for they know not what they do." Can you tell somebody, "You've done me wrong, but I forgive you," oh, glory to God, and then you throw it in the sea of forgetfulness. It doesn't come back like a jack-in-the box, but it's thrown in the sea of forgetfulness, never to come back again.

I'm glad this morning that Jesus died for your sins, and my sins, and for the sins of the world – oh, glory to God - blood running down from His hands and His feet. They pierced Him in the side! They stretched Him wide! Oh, Lord! They put a crown of thorns on His head! And then - oh, glory to God - when they thought He wanted water, they put vinegar on a sponge and put it to His mouth! Oh, Lord! Why did He do it? He did it for you, and He did it for you, and you, and you, and you, and you, and me, and all of us! And for the sins of the world! I'm glad! I'm glad! And then they took Him down off that cross, and they laid Him in a borrowed tomb, oh, glory to God! A cold, dark place! When I was in Israel, I saw it. It was a cold, dark place. There was no light in there, nothing living in there, but they laid Him in a borrowed tomb, and all day Saturday, and all night Saturday night, He lay there, He lay there! Oh, glory to God! But early Sunday morning, the angels rolled the stone away. My Savior was laying there all day Saturday and Saturday night. Then He got up! I see Him now! Getting up! He didn't stumble up like a sleepy man, but He got up with all power! All power was in His hands! He got up! He stood up! The angels had rolled the stone away! He stepped out, all power! I can see Him shouting now, saying, "I've got the victory over the grave! I've got the victory over the devil! I've got the victory over what he's tried!" And I see Jesus stepping out with all power! We, too, one day, are going to have to step out on His Word!

I want to tell you today, as I try to close, it seems like we're having a good time! It seems like the Church Age is going to go on forever. But let me tell you, we don't know; He could come right now! We don't know; He could come right now! We don't know; He could come at this moment! And I want to encourage you today, have your house in order! Have your mind on Him! Have your joy not coming from marijuana, not coming from alcohol, but have your joy coming from the Joy-giver! Oh, Lord! Oh, glory to God! As I close here, Jesus got on a cloud! Oh, glory to God! You might say, "Brother Pastor, why would you say that?" He got on a cloud! He got on a cloud, and He went all the way back! He went all the way back to glory! I'm glad today! I'd have been just like the disciples! I'd have been saying, "Lord, why would You leave me all by myself? I'm binding together with You!" Jesus got on the cloud and went all the way, all the way to glory! But He didn't leave us all by ourselves! Oh, glory to God! He left us with Something... Something... Something! Something! Something! I'm not by myself today, for He left us with Something! He sent It down all the way from heaven! He sent down the power of the Holy Ghost! He sent It down! I'm glad today that I have the Holy Ghost! Moving on the inside! I say to you today, if you don't have It, you're missing something. If you don't have that Something that turns, like somebody said, "I can feel the fire-wheel turning!"

Glory! Hallelujah! You ought to say, "Glory Hallelujah" to Jesus, your King! The Lord of Lords! My all in all! I'm glad this morning! You ought to have a joy today that the world didn't give and the world can't take away! You ought to have a joy of knowing what Jesus said! Binding together in the name of Jesus! I'm glad today, we have the victory today, not in man, but we have the victory in the Lord!

If you're here today and you don't have that Something, you can come now. Come to Jesus. Today is your day. Jesus is calling to you. If you have not accepted Jesus as your personal Savior, you can come now. You can accept Jesus right now, if you pray this prayer with me:

"Father God, I know that I am a sinner and my sins have separated me from You. Father, please forgive me right now. I want to turn away from my sinful life and turn toward You. I believe that Your Son, Jesus Christ, died on the cross for my sins, and on the third day, You raised Him from the dead, and now He is at Your right hand. I invite Jesus to come into my heart and become the Lord of my life from this day forward. Please send Your Holy Spirit to help me obey You, and to do Your will for the rest of my life. In Jesus' name I pray, Amen."

TOGETHERNESS
Amos 3:1-8

Glory to God! Isn't it wonderful that we can praise Him? If you would, turn in your Bibles today to the third chapter of Amos this morning, the first Sunday of the new year. As I was going over notes last night, and had been going over notes all week long, the Spirit of God was dealing with me in terms of what I might share today. We see this morning, and we see that all this year, and this is only the 7th of January, that there are a lot of things going on. Just within the last seven days, we have noticed, even in our own world, there is a lot going on. As I have been praying this week, have been seeking the Lord and asking God to use me for His glory, the Spirit spoke to me and said that we are not together in a lot of areas. Mainly, we are not together as Christians. Those ones, when I say Christians, those ones that have accepted the Lord Jesus Christ as Lord and Savior of their lives. As the Spirit of God has been dealing with me, I've come to the conclusion today that the only way that God's people can accomplish the things that God intends for us to accomplish is that we must be together.

The Word says, in Amos, chapter 3, beginning at the first verse, and it reads to us today:

1. Hear this word that the LORD hath spoken against you, O children of Israel, against the whole family which I brought up from the land of Egypt, saying,
2. You only have I known of all the families of the earth: therefore I will punish you for all your iniquities.
3. Can two walk together, except they be agreed?
4. Will a lion roar in the forest, when he hath no prey? will a young lion cry out of his den, if he have taken nothing?
5. Can a bird fall in a snare upon the earth, where no gin is for him? shall one take up a snare from the earth, and have taken nothing at all?
6. Shall a trumpet be blown in the city, and the people not be afraid? shall there be evil in a city, and the LORD hath not done it?
7. Surely the Lord GOD will do nothing, but he revealeth his secret unto his servants the prophets.

8. The lion hath roared, who will not fear? the Lord GOD hath spoken, who can but prophesy?

I was thinking this week that there are a lot of things that are not together. A young man, and should I say, at least several persons have come to me this week, and they have devastating things in their lives. You might say, "Well, there are others that are going through things." Sure, everybody is going through something. But when I say 'devastation,' that means to the point, almost, of no return. I believe today that there is an answer to the problems of devastation. I believe today that there is nothing too hard for God. I believe today, as the Word has said, as our Sunday School Lesson has implied today, that even Jesus, with all of His glory, with all of His power given to Him by His Father, even Jesus showed and recognized that all that He had done did not come from His majesty, but it came from the Word of God, from the Scriptures that had to be fulfilled. And here we see today, the Word of God must be fulfilled, even in this hour, even in this hour that we're in, the 7th of January, the Word of God must be fulfilled. As we look around today, we can see that the Word of God is being fulfilled in many different ways. I'm happy today. I'm happy because the Word of God is being fulfilled in my own life. For I can testify that I have a joy that the world didn't give, and the world can't take away. I can rejoice in the fact today that the Lord is truly a healer. Not only just a Healer of the body, but He is a Healer of the mind.

The Scripture says, in verse 3 of Amos 3, "Can two walk together, except they be agreed?" We have seen this past year, many who thought they were together. But they weren't together. The book of Acts says they were together, on one accord, and the doors of the jail flew open for Brother Peter. We see that they were together on the day of Pentecost and three thousand souls came to the Lord because of that one message that Peter preached. We could go on and on with the accounts of what happens when people come together. We can see how God moves because of that oneness, or because of that togetherness. Yesterday, Sister Brown and I went around and knocked on doors and gave out flyers about our church services. Maybe she's not aware of it, but that was togetherness. Because of that togetherness, we are going to see a move of God like never before.

This morning, on my way to the church building, I drove around that area. I just drove in that area, and I made the sign of the cross as I drove through that area, knowing and believing that's a harvest there. The Word says, "Truly the harvest is ripe, but the laborers are few." He says, "Go ye out into the harvest, and sow in the harvest." Yesterday was a time of sowing in the harvest. We might not see all of those coming as we think that they might come, but God will send them when He will. I had said that I had tried to get in that area for years, and I had never gotten there. But on yesterday, in the rain, with the big umbrella, the California umbrella, we were out doing the work of the Lord. I'm grateful to God today, that if we lift Him up, He will draw all men. I'm grateful to God today, all that we need is from the Lord. Let us pray at this time.

Our Father, we come to You this morning, we pray that You would use these lips of clay. Not my will, but Thy will be done. Oh, heavenly Father, as we come today, we come, Lord God, preparing our hearts and our minds for the sacraments today. We come, Lord God, believing that this time that You've given us is a time for restoring, a time for getting back to the basics. It's a time, Lord God, for getting back to the foundation of what our church is all about. It's a time, Lord God, of recognizing that faith and hope of what we believe. And Father, we praise You today, we praise You, for You have all power. Now Lord, we commit this day to You. Open up our eyes and open up our ears that we might be receptive to Your Word and Your will. Oh, heavenly Father, let the Word of God be an encouragement to our hearts and our minds. We pray in Jesus's name, Amen.

We see this morning, as the Scripture says, where there is not friendship, there can be no fellowship. I'm glad today that we have friendship here, and because of friendship, we can have fellowship.

Psalm 34:3 says, "Magnify the Lord with me, and let us exalt his name together."
Ezra 4:3 says, "Together, we'll build unto the Lord."
Luke 15:6 says, "He calleth together his friends and neighbors, saying, Rejoice with me; for I have found my sheep which was lost."

Philippians 1:27 says, "Striving together for the faith of the gospel."
Colossians 2:2 says, "being knit together in love."
Philippians 3:17 says, "be followers together of me."

Paul presents his brethren and himself as an example, for he says, "Brethren, be ye followers together of me, and mark them which walk so as ye have for us as an example." For he explains himself by their regard to Christ and heaven. For our conversation, Paul says, is in heaven. It's a wonderful testimony, to have a conversation in heaven. It's a wonderful testimony to get on the phone and to get with one another, and to talk about the things above. It is a wonderful testimony, and it's a wonderful thing that when God's people can come together, on one accord, we can see a move of God. This world is not our home, but a Christian's home is in heaven. It is good having fellowship with those who have fellowship with Christ. And it is good having conversation with those who have a conversation in heaven. We look for the Savior from heaven. We expect to be happy, and glorify Him there. Who shall change our bodies, that they may be fashioned like unto His glorious body? There is a glory reserved for the saints, and that glory is written down in heaven. We were singing a song on last Sunday, "I have a new name written down in glory, and that name is mine, mine, all mine." I'm glad today. I'm glad that we have a new name. I have several tapes from the ministry of Bishop Patterson, who passed away this week. In his last message to the church, he said we need to get back to the basics. He said we need to get back to where women would recognize that the man is the head of the family. He said we need to get back to the basics where the children would respect their elders. We need to get back to the basics where, not only is prayer is trying to come about and be put back into school, but prayer ought to be put back into the home. We ought to get back to the basics, where men and women used to have respect for one another. But they don't have respect for anybody anymore, not even their own selves.

I'm mindful today, of a year or so ago. There was a lady who was a member of our church. She had three or four kids. One particular Sunday, she sent her daughter back into the office to ask me to post something on the bulletin board. When the young lady came back, she said to me, "Pastor," and she gave this woman's first name. "She wants to know if you would post this on the bulletin board." I said to this young lady, "Who did you say wanted to post it?" And she went on to give me the first name. And I said to her, "Who is this that you're referring to?" And she said, "It's my mother." I said to her, "Let me tell you, as long as you are part of this church, as long as you know me, I never want to hear you address your mother by her first name."

So the girl gave me the information, and a few days later the mother came to me and asked me, "What do you mean, chastising my daughter?" I said to her, "I only told her what God loves." And let me tell you today, when you tell somebody what God loves, it has to be the truth. I'm glad today. I'm glad that I'm standing on the wall today. I'm glad that I'm on my post, telling a dying world that the wages of sin is death, but the gift of God is eternal life. Somebody would say this morning, "Where are all the masses of people? Where are the ones that attend our church?" I want to tell you today that the Lord is purging, and He's moving out, and He's sending in. Going back to this lady, she said to me, "I don't want anybody chastising my daughter. I don't want anybody saying anything to my kids about what's right and what's wrong." I said to her, "Sister, I don't have any problem with what you say. But I want to tell you, if she calls you by your first name around me, I'm going to tell her like I told her the other day, she better call you 'Mom,' 'Sister So-and-so,' or whatever, but she better not call you by your first name." The sister said to me, "Well, I'm not coming back to the church any more." I said, "Well, that's your choice, but I'm going to tell you what thus saith the Lord." But let me tell you, six months later, this girl, I was told, they saw her walking the streets of Union Avenue.

Oh, I'm glad today. I'm glad that when two come together in agreement, we can see a move of God like never before. Oh, as my mind reflects this morning, my grandson, just a couple weeks ago, he got an earring in his ear. And I want to tell you today, I didn't like it then and I don't like it now. I saw him a couple days ago, and he had this earring in his ear. Only five years old! And I want to tell you, his attitude was so negative, it was unreal. He didn't have any joy, as a five-year-old should have. He didn't have any peace as a five-year-old should have. As I looked at him, I was grieved in my spirit. But let me tell you today, that's what happens when ones don't agree. The devil will come in and he will destroy. He will tear down something that has been built up for years and years.

I'm glad this morning that the foundation of Christ, the devil can't tear it down. For Jesus said, "Upon this rock, I build my church, and the very gates of hell cannot prevail against it." Oh, I'm glad this morning. I'm glad that the church, Jesus said, it wasn't the building. I'm glad this morning that Jesus said the church wasn't the cathedral in Rome, or wherever the big cathedrals might be. But the church is the baptized body of believers, assembled together, coming together to worship the name of the true and living God. That's what the church is today. And I'm glad this morning that we are the church of the living God. We can come together and lift up His holy name. I'm glad this morning that man didn't call me, but I was called by the Lord.

Amos said, concerning the second prophecy, they called to hear an answer. He said, "I will punish you for all your iniquities." We can see today that there are many that are being punished because of their iniquities. I'm glad this morning, oh, glory to God, that I'm not the avenger this morning. I'm glad today that I'm not the judge -- oh, glory to God -- but God is the Judge, the One that sits high and looks low. I'm glad this morning -- oh, glory to God -- that I can't put anything on anybody to make them do what I want them to do! But we have a free choice. We can serve the Lord, or not serve the Lord. We can worship over here, or we can worship over there. Oh, I'm glad today! I'm glad that I have a message today, and it didn't come from man, but it came from God. Oh, I'm glad this morning, as we agree today -- oh, glory to God -- first of all, that I'm saved -- oh, glory to His name! We can agree today that I'm filled with the Spirit of God. Jesus said, "I work the works of Him that sent me while it is day. When night cometh, no man can work." Jesus was saying we must work together right here. We must work! Oh, glory to God! I'm glad this morning! Oh, praise His holy name! I'm doing the work of an evangelist! I'm doing the work of a missionary! I'm doing the work of a teacher this morning! Oh, bless God's name.

I remember a few years ago -- oh, glory to God! -- when we used to meet in a house on Sunday morning, oh, bless His name!

And in that service, I didn't have a pulpit! Oh, glory to God! We didn't have any chairs. We used to sit around -- oh, glory to God! -- on box tops, on wooden crates, and I would stand and talk about Jesus. Oh, I'm glad today, I'm still standing on the wall, talking about the Lord! I'm glad today, for togetherness! I'm glad that I have a message that the world didn't give and the world can't take away! I'm glad! Oh, thank You, Jesus! Oh, glory to God! If it weren't but two, I would say a word for the Lord! I'm glad today, I can go on all the way! Oh, bless God's holy name! Thank You, Jesus, for what You're doing!

I want to tell you today, I know we didn't have testimony service, but I want to testify today. I have joy! -- oh, glory to God! -- that I haven't had in years! I have peace! Oh, glory to God! I can lay down -- oh, glory to God! -- and I don't have to worry about somebody coming and maybe doing something to me. I can lay down -- oh, glory to God! -- my body, knowing that everything is going to be all right. Let me tell you today, when you're tied up in the Lord, He will -- oh, glory to God! -- make everything all right! I feel something now! It's coming down from heaven today! Oh, glory to God! I know what it is today! It's the Word of God! I want to tell you today, if you don't know the Lord, if you have not been tied up, wrapped up, in His Word, you may not understand what I'm talking about. You ought to have the Word of God! David said, "Thy Word, have I hid in my heart, that I might not sin against thee." Thy Word! -- oh, glory to God! -- it is a lamp to my feet and a light to my path! Thy Word today -- oh, glory to God! -- is all that we need!

Let us put our hands in God's hand. Let us know that the Lord is -- He is today! -- in control. I feel something now. The message today is not only for you, but it is for me! Oh, glory to God!

Thank You, Jesus, for what You're doing! Thank You, Jesus, for the pouring out! Thank You, Jesus, I can call on You today! Thank You, Jesus! Oh, glory to God!

As I move on here this morning, togetherness, standing on the Word! Togetherness, standing on the Word of God! Let me tell you this morning, I love the Lord today, because -- oh, glory to God! -- the Lord is good! The Lord is merciful today! The

Lord is gracious today. I remember, as a boy growing up, there was something about the Word, the Word of God! It was something about the preached Word. Let me tell you today, I was born in a preacher's home. All I ever heard was the preached Word of God. Let me tell you today, once you get tied up in the Lord, you have a love for His Word. Jesus said this morning in the Sunday School lesson, "It's not My will, but it's the will of God. It's not My word, but it's the Word of God." I'm glad today, for the mighty Lamb of God. The Word! You ought to be happy about it! The Word of God, wherever it's going forth, you ought to want to be right there. The Word of God is the only thing that can control our lives. It's the only thing that can turn this world around. I'm glad today, so glad, so glad! I'm so glad today, I've got not just a religion this morning, but I've got a testimony down on the inside. I'm glad, so glad, so glad today! I'm going on with the Lord! I don't know about you today -- oh, glory to God!

Can two walk together, except they be agreed? Second Corinthians 6:14-18 says, "Keep to your own selves. Do not leave Christians and join with unbelievers." That indicates that some Corinthians were joining with heathen in idolatry practices that would lead them to apostasy.

I'm glad today. I'm glad today! I'm standing on the Word! Oh, glory to God! Thank You, Jesus! Oh, bless His name today! Everywhere I go, I can tell somebody that the Lord is good! I can tell somebody -- oh, glory to His name! -- that Jesus is all in all. Fellowship -- oh, glory to God! -- with one another. Communion together. Break bread -- oh, glory to God! -- and drink His blood. He sent His body down -- oh, glory to God! -- wrapped up -- oh, glory to God! -- in sinful flesh, that we might have life, and life more abundantly. I'm glad! I'm glad! I'm glad this morning, I know the Lord! I'm glad today! Oh, bless His name! He went all the way back, all the way to glory! Oh, glory to His name! And He came down with all power! All power, all power was in His hands!

As I close this morning, let me close with this, that Jesus was hanging there on the cross, blood running down from His hands and His feet, but He didn't say a mumbling word. I'm glad! I'm glad! He was together with His Father! Oh, bless His name today! Oh, I feel something now! -- oh, glory to God! --

He was together, as He was hanging there, on the cross, with His Father. Not together with Peter, James or John! He was together with His Father. I'm glad today! When He was hanging there, blood running down from His hands and His feet, all He said was, "Not my will, but Thy will be done."

I'm glad this morning -- oh, glory to God! -- that I've got a message today! -- oh, glory to God! If the world could turn me off or turn me on, they would turn me off right now. But let me tell you today, it doesn't come from man or any other substance. But it comes from God. God will make a way for you. God will -- oh, glory to God! -- I feel something now! I didn't want to go so long, but let me tell you today, it's something about the Word of God! It's something about the Spirit of God! I love the Lord! I love the Lord! I don't know about you today! You ought to love Him everywhere you go! You ought to be able to tell somebody, "What Jesus has done for me, He'll do the same for you. He'll heal your body!" Oh, glory to God! I don't need five pills to get a healing today! I don't need alcohol or dope to get a feeling today! I can feel His Spirit -- oh, glory to God! I don't need gossip today to get my motor going -- oh, glory to God! I don't need a joy pill in the morning to get me going. I wake up with my joy! Oh, glory! Oh, glory to God! It's joy! Jeremiah, the prophet, said, "It's like fire shut up in my bones."

I'm glad this morning -- oh, glory to God! -- as I close here, that Jesus -- oh, glory -- He died that I might have life! He died that you might have life! He shed His blood on Calvary's cross! He didn't have to do it, but He did! Oh, thank You, Lord, thank You, Jesus! We don't need sacrifices! Thank You, Jesus! You were the sacrifice! Thank You, Jesus! -- oh, glory to God! -- I'm glad! I'm glad this morning! -- oh, glory to God! -- that they took Him down off that cross, --oh glory, glory to God -- blood running down from His hands and His feet. But He didn't say a mumbling word. I want to challenge you this morning, oh, bless His name! If you don't believe, look at Jesus, hanging there, on that cross, oh, not this cross, but on His cross -- oh, glory to God! Thank You, Lord, oh, thank You, Lord! It's something about the blood of Jesus.

If you're here this morning, if you need a covering this morning -- oh, glory to God! -- don't cover yourself with a blanket. Don't cover yourself with anything else, but cover yourself with the blood of Jesus. I'm glad. I'm glad this morning! Oh, glory to God! I thank You, Lord, for the Word today! I thank you, Lord, for the Word of God! Oh, glory! Oh, glory! I feel it now! Oh, bless His name, the name of Jesus! They took Him down off that cross! There's something about a cross today! Oh, glory! I don't know about you this morning! Maybe you've been disappointed. Don't you know, that's a cross. Maybe you've been sick in your body, and the doctor said he's going to give you up, that's a cross. Maybe you've not had a place to stay. Don't you know, that's a cross. Maybe you've been lonely. Don't you know, that's a cross. But Jesus said, "I bear your cross, and the cross of the world. All you've got to do is lean on Me. Lean on Me and I will turn your midnights into day! I will give you joy that the world didn't give and the world can't take away."

They took Him down off that cross and placed Him in a borrowed tomb, all day Saturday, and all night Saturday night! Oh, bless the Lord! Oh, glory! He got up, oh, glory, Sunday morning, all power, all power was in His hands! I'm glad today! I've got some power! I can move on when my body gets tired. I've got some power today, though the cross gets heavy, I can go on with the Lord. As I close this morning, look at Jesus, going all the way to Calvary. All the way back, all the way back! All the way back! He went back, all the way, all the way to Calvary! Oh glory, all the way to His Father. But He sent Something -- oh, glory to God! -- that will never leave us nor forsake us. And I'm glad today, that I have that Something, that Something that moves on the inside. That Something that the world didn't give. That Something that didn't come from man. I'm glad today, I'm glad. I'm glad that Jesus sent the Holy Ghost, sent the Comforter, the One that He said would lead us and guide us into all truth and righteousness. Thank You, Lord. Thank You, Jesus. I'm glad this morning!

If you're here today and you haven't received the Lord Jesus as your personal Savior, you need to accept Him right now. All we've got to do is to be instant in season and out of season. As Jesus said, "Be faithful unto death, and I will give you precious things in life."

THE WORK OF THE HOLY SPIRIT
Romans 8:7-10, II Kings 5:11-13

God bless you today. Would you turn with me to Romans, chapter 8, verses 7-10:

7. Because the carnal mind is enmity against God: for it is not subject to the law of God, neither indeed can be.
8. So then they that are in the flesh cannot please God.
9. But ye are not in the flesh, but in the Spirit, if so be that the Spirit of God dwell in you. Now if any man have not the Spirit of Christ, he is none of his.
10. And if Christ be in you, the body is dead because of sin; but the Spirit is life because of righteousness.

I want to preach to you for a few minutes from that verse, "The Work of the Holy Spirit." Now turn to Second Kings, chapter 5, verses 11-13.

11. But Naaman was wroth, and went away, and said, Behold, I thought, He will surely come out to me, and stand, and call on the name of the LORD his God, and strike his hand over the place, and recover the leper.
12. Are not Abana and Pharpar, rivers of Damascus, better than all the waters of Israel? may I not wash in them, and be clean? So he turned and went away in a rage.
13. And his servants came near, and spake unto him, and said, My father, if the prophet had bid thee do some great thing, wouldest thou not have done it? how much rather then, when he saith to thee, Wash, and be clean?

It is always crossing my mind, as children of God, we act as if there is no hope. We act as if there is no life. We act as if we have no faith. It's kind of discouraging today, to look around, and I'm talking about the Christian church right now; the world, they have their own pattern, they have their own way of dealing with things, but I'm talking about the Christians today, the ones who say they have been baptized and washed in the blood of the Lamb, the ones who say they have been filled with the Holy

Ghost and fire. As children of God, we act as if there is no hope! We act as if there is no life, and no faith, and as if we are on this journey all by ourselves. But let me tell you today, Jesus, the Son of God, your Savior and my Savior, the One who took away the sins of the world, He endured the cross. And He endured the cross as an example for you and me, that we too have to endure a cross. I preached last year the sermon, "No Cross, No Crown." You must bear a cross if you're going to bear a crown. Oh, bless His name today! Oh, look at the devil, and how he or she, not just he-devil, but how he or she uses things to keep us from under the protection of God. What a waste that is. What a loss that is, for us not to realize that we have been bought with a price. And that price was Jesus Christ, who said to us, "Take up your cross, and follow me."

The other day I was in the company of some men. One man was saying that he was in some kind of sport. This man went on to say that he was doing well, he had gone through all of the physical training, he had gotten himself ready to do great in this sport that he was in. This other friend that he knew -- I didn't know the other guy very well -- he went on to tell him, "If you're in that sport, you better get an insurance policy. You better get a policy because you could get your legs broken. You could get yourself really hurt. You better get yourself some protection." This man said, "I'm only 25 years old." He said that he didn't feel that anything was going to happen to him because he was in good physical shape. I spoke to this man that was in this sport a little later, and I said to him, "Don't get discouraged. Regardless to what's going on and what you're dealing with, don't get discouraged. Don't let the negativity of this man, who has tried to tell you to get an insurance policy, and that you're not physically fit, and that you can't get well, and that you can't be healed, and that you can't be blessed -- don't get discouraged, because the devil said you don't have any friends. Don't get discouraged, but stay on the course." I want to encourage you this morning, don't get discouraged. Even though the devil would tell you all kinds of things about what others are doing and not doing, don't you get discouraged. You keep your hands in God's hand, and let Him make the way out of no way, and I know that He will.

Here we see this morning, as Romans 8:9 says, "But ye are not in the flesh, but in the Spirit, if so be that the Spirit of God dwell in you. Now if any man have not the Spirit of Christ, he is none of his." I want to tell you also today, that there are many today who are none of His. There are many today who don't have the Spirit of Christ.

Many classes we have in our land, and even in our own community. The sociologists have informed us that we have three classes of people: a lower class, a middle class and an upper class. We realize that according to this classification, there are classes within these. In India alone, there are four basic classes, and on the other hand, there are about two thousand sub-classes. But actually, out of the many classes we have in the world, there are only two classes of people: those who are after the Spirit and those who are after the flesh. There are those people who remain in the state in which they were born, consulting only what they were and what they believe. Then there are those that are born in the Spirit. For Jesus said to Nicodemus that he must be born again. "Oh," Nicodemus said to Jesus, "How can I be born again when I'm an old man? I'm a man of age, and how can I be born again?" And Jesus made it plain to him that he must be born of the water and of the Spirit.

Again, our classes consist of those who are carnally minded and those who are spiritually minded. I want to encourage you today, are you spiritually minded? Are you doing the work of an evangelist? Are you doing the work that God has set forth in your life? The carnal minded man is paralyzed. "What do you mean, Brother Pastor?" I'm saying that the carnal minded is paralyzed in his thinking. He always has the negative. He's always wanting to put someone down. But let me tell you today, the spiritually minded person is life and peace. The work of the Holy Spirit, as it works in our lives, promises that Jesus said that He would not leave us nor forsake us. Oh, we see today that the carnal minded man has his impulses. Sometimes he is touched and moved by what appears to be divine instincts. Oh, I'm mindful today that the natural man today can read this Bible from cover to cover, but he can't understand what it says! Oh, he knows the words. He knows the 'thees' and 'thous' but his intellect is limited. But the Spiritually minded person sees this as the Book of books. Somebody would say today, "You mean to tell me that you believe that a donkey spoke to a man?" Oh, yes, I do! "You mean to tell me you believe that God prepared a fish big enough to swallow a man?" Oh, yes, I do! "You mean to tell me that you believe that God made it rain 40 days and 40 nights and destroyed all of civilization?" Oh, yes, I do! Oh, glory to God! I believe it because of the spiritual insight that God has given us when we came into His fullness.

You who are spiritually minded must not cease renewing your faith, shining up your armor, keeping your shoes shod for the fight against sin that Satan is ever on. Oh, you that are here today, I'm glad that we've got missionaries and preachers and others who know your calling here today, because otherwise, you wouldn't understand. But you that are here today, you can understand what thus saith the Lord. For it says that he who is after the flesh cannot please God. The flesh can't please Him. But as stated in the text, is none of Christ's. He is not a member of His body, not a child in His family, and not a subject of His kingdom. Oh, I'm glad about that. We have ones preaching religions today, saying that all that you've got to do is come over here, and believe in this type of religion, and all of these others, and you can make it in. But I want to tell you today, the carnal minded will not enter the kingdom of heaven. Oh, we all are going to stand before the judgment seat of Christ, but all will not make it in. The Word says that he who dies outside the Spirit of Christ will not enter the kingdom of God. But I'm glad that I'm going to make it in, because I have the Spirit of Christ that dwelleth within me. Somebody said it's like rivers of living water flowing out of my belly! Oh, bless His name today!

Consider today, the Spirit of Christ. The whole Scriptures declare that there is only one true and living God. But in the unity of the Godhead, there are three, whom we call persons. Their names describe the manner of existence among themselves which is above all knowledge to understand. One faith, one baptism, and one Holy Ghost. The Divine person that we speak of is called the Holy Spirit. The Holy Spirit has understanding and It has wisdom.

I was sharing during Bible Studies on Tuesday night, that, as a Christian, you ought to have the gift of discernment. Somebody said to me, "Oh, what kind of gift is that?" I tell you today, if you don't have the gift of discernment, you're headed for some rocky roads. I want to tell you today, it's something about the Holy Spirit or the Holy Ghost, when He moves on the inside. Jesus said It will lead you and guide you into all truth and righteousness. Oh, I'm glad today that It teaches us. I'm glad that It guides us. I'm glad that It convinces us. I'm glad that It renews us. I'm glad that It speaks to us, and I'm glad that It shows us. I'm glad that It calls us and I'm glad that It sends us. Somebody would say today, "What do you mean, Brother Pastor?" I'm saying that you can't draw yourself. I can draw you, but only for a little while. But let me tell you, when the Spirit of God draws you, It keeps you! Oh, bless God's holy name!

Somebody said to me just last week, "I've been with the Lord about 15 or 20 years," and then they went on to say to me, "I've started drinking again and started smoking again." But let me tell you today, I believe that when God calls you out, He doesn't let you go back out there. I believe that when God puts His Holy Ghost, moving on the inside, you can sing like they used to sing, "I've been running for Jesus a long time, and I'm not tired yet." I don't know about you today, but if you've been born again, not just of the water, but of the Spirit, you ought to have a testimony that you know that God that liveth, and He liveth within. Oh, I'm glad today. I'm glad for the Holy Ghost today. I'm glad for what He does in our lives.

As I move on here this morning, Peter told Ananias that he had not lied unto men, but he had lied unto God. Jesus told His apostles, "Teach all nations." Oh, glory to God! Christians have the Spirit of Christ. The most dangerous area of this to maintain is that the influence of the Spirit is not to be expected now. But let me tell you today, you ought to have the Spirit of God, moving down on the inside. You ought to have something today! Somebody said that if I didn't have Christ in my life, I'd have nothing at all. But I'm glad today, that I've got Christ! Oh, glory to God! Everywhere you go, you ought to let your light shine! You ought to tell somebody, "I know the Lord has been good to me! I know the Lord has brought me from a mighty long way!" I know the Lord -- oh, bless His name today! -- will keep me and guide me into all truth and righteousness! I don't know about you today! You ought to have Something that will put running in your feet! You ought to have Something! Oh, glory to God! When men say all kinds of things against you, you ought to have Something that will make you hold your peace.

Oh, I'm glad today! I'm glad for the Holy Spirit, moving and guiding! I'm glad this morning! Oh, glory to God! I don't have to wait on It! Jesus said, "If I don't go, It won't come!" Let me tell you today, you ought to have something! Oh, bless His name! Regardless to what the heartaches or what the cross might be, you ought to have Something -- oh, glory to God! -- that will lift you up. Oh, glory to God! When you're not feeling good, you ought to have Something moving on the inside! I'm glad today! I don't need the medicine cabinet! I've got a medicine that no drug store sells! I'm not knocking medicine today, I'm simply saying, you can take medicine in a moderate way and everything will be all right. You can have surgery and God can use the doctor -- oh, glory to God! -- to heal your body! I'm saying today, you don't have to rely on man today! Stand on His Word today, and He will, He will!

The Spirit of God is called the Spirit of truth. We only know the truth by having the Spirit. Those early Christians who received it in the beginning, and even those who receive it now, have power! What kind of power do you have today? Do you have power that you can lay hands on the sick and they will recover? I've come to the conclusion today, we can bind all kinds of devils, but you've got to have some power to know what kind of devil it is! I had a lady tell me just a few weeks ago, that she's got multiple sclerosis, and she went into a church just a few weeks ago. When she went in, she was in a wheelchair. As soon as she rolled in, she went up for prayer, to pray for salvation. And four or five dived around her, and began to rebuke foul spirits. But let me tell you today, you ought to know what kind of spirit it is! You ought to have a discernment today, to be able to tell the Lord, I'm doing my Father's will, just like Jesus said! Not my will, but Thy will be done! Can you tell somebody, "It's not my will, why I act the way I act." It's not my will, Lord, why I do what I do, but it's my Father's will -- oh, glory to God! -- that's working in me! Oh, bless His name! The Holy Spirit!

Let me give you some examples today. The Holy Spirit works like this, being everywhere. The Spirit said, wherever I go, the Spirit goes with me. The Holy Spirit knew that Jesus was to be born by Mary. The Holy Spirit saw Paul as a revealer! The Spirit itself beareth witness with my Spirit that we are children of God, Romans 8:16. Oh, I'm glad today! You ought to be able to try the spirit by the Spirit! Not the devil's spirit, but the Spirit of God! The greatest work of the Holy Spirit is to save men. And we need Him now! We need Him in this hour! Oh, glory to God!

Let me move on here today! I don't care what the world does! God is in control of this world! Oh, bless His name! The 4th chapter of Acts gives us the miracles of Peter which were done by the Holy Spirit. He healed a man of a disease and the rulers came forward for him to restrain all his works in the name of Jesus. There's power today in that name! I'm glad! I'm glad! I'm glad today! That Holy Ghost power, moving right now!

Let me tell you today, if I could testify for a moment. Oh, bless His name! In Second Kings -- oh, glory to God! -- the Scripture we read today, it said there was a man by the name of Naaman. Oh, bless God's name! This man had a disease. I don't know about you today, if you've ever been sick. I'm not talking about a headache, but I'm talking about really sick! Oh, bless God! Look at this man, Naaman, oh, bless His name! The Word says he had a disease and the doctors didn't have a cure for it. The Word says Naaman knew -- oh, glory to God! -- he knew what was needed! Oh, bless His name! The Word says there was a slave girl that lived in Naaman's house, and one day Mrs. Naaman -- oh, bless God! -- told her husband, "Honey, I heard the slave girl in our home talk about a man of God. And maybe he can cure you of your disease. Maybe he can cure you of that infirmity that you've got." Oh, glory to God! Naaman said, -- oh, bless God's name today -- "Where is this man that might be able to help me? How many did you say that he healed?" And Mrs. Naaman said, "Let me tell you, I don't know how many, but why don't you try? You've tried everything. You've tried the doctors and they haven't done any good. You've tried the physicians, every one of them, and they've done you no good. You've tried every medication and they've done you no good."

I want to tell you today, the world needs to try Jesus! Broken homes today need to try Jesus! The jails today are full on every side, they need to try Jesus! Oh, bless His name today! Wherever sin is raging today, they need to try Jesus! I guarantee you today, there's no failure in the Lord! We fail and come short of the glory of God. Look at Naaman, going to the prophet -- oh, glory to God! -- all diseased -- oh, bless His name! He had a disease and there was no cure. The Word says, he went to the prophet and the prophet told him, "I want you to go down to the Jordan River. I want you go down and I want you to dip seven times." Let me tell you today, if we be obedient, not to man, but to the Word of God, everything, everything! will be alright! Let me tell you, whatever the burden might me, if you stand on the Word, everything! You won't need dope! You won't need crack! You won't need alcohol! You won't need lying and cheating! But everything will be alright! Naaman, the Word says, went down to the river. I'm glad today -- oh, glory to God! Why would the prophet send this man down to a dirty river, a muddy river -- oh, glory to God! Let me tell you today, the things of man are different from the things of God! Oh, glory! Oh, glory! You ought to have it today, moving on the inside! I feel it now! I feel the Holy Ghost, moving all on the inside of me! I feel like preaching now! Oh, I go in Revival all next month, I'm going four more times this year! But I'm geared up with His Word! I'm geared up with His power!

If you will look at Brother Naaman, going down to the river -- oh, bless God's name! Something about the river, it's something about the water and it's something about the blood. The Word says, he went down to the river. Let me tell you today, you ought to be obedient! Don't do as I do, but do as the Word says! I'm supposed to be an example for you -- oh, glory to God! -- but stand on the Word! If you see me falling, don't fall with me! Stand on the Word today! Oh, glory! The Word says Naaman went down to the river. He went on out there, in the river. He went down the first time -- oh, glory to God! – and nothing happened! You ought to be obedient to the Word of God! He went down the second time and nothing happened. You ought to know today, whatever the Word says, do what it says. Jesus' mother said, "Whatever He tells you to do, you ought to do it." Don't question what the Word of God says. The third time, Naaman went down in the river nothing happened to him -- oh, glory to God! The fourth time, he went down in the river, nothing happened. The fifth time he went down in the river, nothing happened. The sixth time, he went down in the river, nothing happened. But let me tell you today, if you wait on the Lord, He will, He will, He will make a way out of no way! He will, oh, glory to God! I know I'm right about it! Let me tell you, look at Brother Naaman! He went on in the seventh time. The Word says, when he came up, he looked at his hands and they looked new. He looked at his feet and they were, too. He looked at his face and it was clean.

I'm glad! I'm glad! Do what the Word says, and everything will be all right! Oh, glory! You can be new today! You can be cleansed today, in the power of the Lord, and the power of His blood! Look at Jesus, hanging there, on the cross, blood running down -- oh, glory! I feel my help now! Oh, Lord! Oh, Lord! Blood running down from His hands and His feet! I love the Word! I love the preached Word! I can feel it now! I'm preaching to myself now! Oh, bless His name! I don't know about you, you ought to have a sermon that ought to minister to yourself sometimes! Oh, look at Jesus, hanging there, blood running down from His hands and His feet. But He didn't say a mumbling word, but "Father, my Father!" Do you have a Father today that you can call on when burdens get heavy? Oh, glory to God! Do you have a Father you can call on when you don't have any money? Do you have a Father you can call on when you don't have any friends? I'm glad today! Jesus said, "My Father and I are one." I'm glad, I'm glad! Jesus, He was hanging there, oh, glory! Oh glory! I feel it now! I feel like shouting all out of my clothes! Oh, Lord! Oh, Lord! Jesus said, "I give My body! They didn't take My life! I gave it so they might have life!" I'm glad today! I'm glad! Look at Jesus, hanging there, oh, bless His name! Oh, bless His name! Jesus said, "I could call ten thousand angels to My rescue! I'm not going to call anybody, I know what My Father's will is." Sometimes, you ought to not call anybody. You ought to get on your knees and talk with the Lord. You ought to tell the Lord all about the problem.

Look at Jesus. They took Him off the cross, and they placed Him in a borrowed tomb. And early Sunday morning, He got up with all power. All power was in His hands! I can stand on His power today! You ought to be able to stand on the Word of God. Thank You, Lord! Thank You, Lord! Thank You, Lord, for helping me. I can stand on Your Word today! Oh, I'm glad! Hallelujah! Oh, bless His name! I'm glad today that Jesus went all the way back. I'm glad! Oh, I'm glad! You can't imagine how glad I am. I'm glad! My father died a year ago this May, he left me. But Jesus said, "I'll never leave you or forsake you." I'm glad today! I'm glad today! I've got something that the world didn't give and the world can't take away! Oh, Lord! Oh, Lord! Look at Jesus, going back, all the way to glory! But He sent Something, Something! Oh, I'm glad! Power! Wonder-working power! His power is real today! I'm glad! I'm glad! Soul-saving power! I challenge you today, if you don't have power, you need to call on the name of the Lord! If gossip is getting your attention, you need to call on the name of the Lord! If everybody is doing everything to you, you need to call on the Lord! I'm glad! Oh, I'm glad!

I'm trying to close here, Lord, but I'm glad! I've got something moving on the inside of me! I've got something, oh, glory to God! I don't know about you today! I feel like shouting! Oh, glory! Jesus! Oh, my Jesus! I love Him today! I love Him! Do you love my Jesus? Do you love my Jesus? Do you love my Jesus? Do you love my Jesus? Thank You, Lord, for the Holy Ghost! I'm glad! I'm glad! I'm glad today, He went all the way back! All the way to Calvary and all the way to glory, in my Father's house! Jesus said, "I go to prepare a place for you." I'm glad! We're in the land of the dying, getting ready for the land of the living. We're not living over here! Don't worry about your body! You're going to have a new body! I'm glad! Oh, I'm glad! I'm going to have a new walk! Oh, glory! My name, written down, not in a history book, but in God's book! I'm glad! Oh, I'm glad! Thank You, Lord, oh, thank You, Lord, oh, thank You, Lord, thank You, Lord, for what You're doing right now! Thank You, Lord, I can call on You morning, noon, and night! Your line is never busy! Thank You, Lord, oh, thank You, Jesus. Oh, bless His name! Bless His name! Hallelujah! Hallelujah! Hallelujah! Hallelujah! Hallelujah! Oh, Hallelujah! Hallelujah! Oh, Hallelujah! I'm glad today! I'm glad! I'm so glad Jesus lifted me!

If you've never accepted Jesus as your personal Savior, you can come now.

GOD ALWAYS HAS A WAY OUT
Matthew 16:17-20

We want to share just a few moments this morning, with you today. If you would turn with me in your Bibles to the book of Matthew, the 16th chapter, verses 17, 18, 19 and 20. We ask ourselves today, "Is there a Word from the Lord?" There's always a Word from God. Somebody would say, "How does that Word come?" It does not always come as a lightening bolt. It does not always come as a dream in the night. But God always has a Word for us. God is trying to tell us something. The thing of it is, are we willing to listen to what God has to say? He has so many ways He is trying to get our attention. I just thank and praise the Lord today that God truly is in control.

I want to just take a few moments, if you will allow me today, because I thank God for you that are here. It was no accident that God fixed it so we would be here at this hour. I've come to the conclusion today that God pre-destined or pre-ordained that we would be here at this time. We must remember today that there are many who don't want to hear what the Word says, but they want to hear what makes their ears feel good. There are many right in the churches today, if I were preaching a gospel that said you could smoke, and drink, and be merry; if I were preaching a gospel that said, "Do your own thing, it's alright," I believe our building would be full right now. If I were telling people that there was no hell, that this was heaven right here, and all you had to do was look within yourself, and you had all the answers, I believe that our church building right now would be filled. Society is looking to hear something smooth. They're looking to hear kind words, and they're looking to hear how good things are, or how good the world is, how at peace the world is today. But let me tell you today, that's one of the biggest lies that Satan could ever do. Jesus said, "When men begin to say, 'Peace, peace,' there is no peace!" For the end is nigh. So there'll never be any more peace until He comes, and He brings peace! I don't care how many summits are going on, or how many trips the President makes to Cambodia or Colombia, there is no peace in this world today. The only peace that we have is within, with Jesus!

A young man yesterday said to me that there's a group that calls themselves Winehearts, or something like that, and they are a cult group. They tell you that you can do the best, and you can be the best, and you can carry on the best because of who you are. I said to him, yes, people feel that way, but it's not who you are. It's who Jesus is! Who is He in your life? What is He doing in your life? What is He doing in your mind? What is He doing when He controls your body? What is He doing when He doesn't allow you to do the things that your flesh would want to do? And that's the bottom line today. Who is Jesus?

St. Matthew, 16th chapter today, verses 17-20, as they read to us this morning:

17. And Jesus answered and said unto him, Blessed art thou, Simon Barjona: for flesh and blood hath not revealed it unto thee, but my Father which is in heaven.
18. And I say also unto thee, That thou art Peter, and upon this rock I will build my church; and the gates of hell shall not prevail against it.
19. And I will give unto thee the keys of the kingdom of heaven: and whatsoever thou shalt bind on earth shall be bound in heaven: and whatsoever thou shalt loose on earth shall be loosed in heaven.
20. Then charged he his disciples that they should tell no man that he was Jesus the Christ.

Let us pray at this time.

Our Father, we come to You this morning, Lord God, and Father, as we look to You today, we look to You as the Author and Finisher of our faith. Oh, heavenly Father, I just want to move out of the way. Use these lips of clay, that we might be hearers and not just hearers only, but doers of Your Word. Oh, heavenly Father, wherever Your Word is going forth today, give power to Your Word. Lord God, we need You now. Oh, heavenly Father, we believe today by faith, You said in Your Word, faith is the substance of things hoped for, the evidence of things not seen. And we have the faith today of a mustard seed cut in fourths, believing that all things will work to our good, for You said, Lord God, that these signs shall follow those who are believers in You, that they shall lay hands on the sick, and they shall recover! Father, we praise You right now, for what You've

done and are doing and going to do, in Jesus' name. Lord God,
let Your Spirit go beyond these walls, let It go into the highways
and byways, and move by Your Spirit, Lord God, to do those
things, Lord God, that are pleasing in Thy sight. In Jesus' name
we pray. Thank God, thank God, thank God.

On the other night, I had a chance to meditate and talk with
the Lord. While I was talking, and the Lord was dealing with
me, I had a dream or a vision. There's something about when
you get away from others, God can begin to deal with you. I can
truly say today, I can understand what Abraham experienced
when God told him to get away from his family and his kindred
and go to a place where God would deal with him. I can see in
my mind why God did that. There are many times we can only
say that God is truly in control. We can see, not only from
Abraham, but we can see that because of his obeying God and
believing God, that God made a promise to him. That promise,
today, that God made to Abraham, we are results of that promise
right now. You might say, "Well, what promise did God make
to Abraham?" God told Abraham He would make him a father
of a nation. There would be so many in that nation, that even the
sands of the seaside would number just that many. We can see
today that we are attributes. We are not blood descendants of
Abraham, but we are descendents of Abraham by faith. And
Abraham was called the father of faith, and we too are grafted
into that family of Abraham, not by blood, but by the promise
that was given to Abraham, and the promise that we have today,
in God's Word.

We can go on this morning and say that even with Moses,
Moses was told to leave his family and to go out to a place where
he would have a relationship, a place where God could talk with
him and let him know that he had to go back to Israel and say to
Pharaoh that God said, "Let My people go." It means God a lot
of times wants to get us away from our families and friends so
God can use us and we can hear what the Lord has to say. I'm
grateful to God that I'm in a position much like that today, that
God has moved me away from others so I can hear what the
Lord has to say, and to do what God wants me to do.

On the other night, as I was seeking the Lord, I had a
strange dream. In that dream, I was doing a meeting in a town.
When I arrived at the airport to be picked up, there was a man

that picked me up there and I didn't know the man, but apparently the man knew me. He said to me, "I'm the one to pick you up." I said to him, "Okay," and we got my baggage, and we got in the car, and off we went to the city that was close by where I was going to be doing the meeting. I said to him, "Where is the pastor?" He said the pastor had died, but that the meeting was going on anyway, and they had gotten another pastor. He mentioned this pastor's name, and I said to him, "Oh, yes, I know him. He's from Los Angeles, isn't he?" And this man said, "Yes." I said, "He's a good preacher." We drove on to where the meetings were. We went to a certain house, and when I got out of the car, this man and I were standing in front of the car. As I looked around, I saw different things happening. I saw people that were loitering or loafing in different parts of the streets, and they were in numbers of fours and fives, and it reminded me of a ghetto situation. They really weren't doing anything, but they were numbered three and four over here, and three and four over there. They were numbered in all kinds of places. They weren't doing anything. They were loafing. They were just there.

I don't know about you. Maybe you've seen ones loafing, or maybe you yourself have been loafing. In other words, they weren't doing anything important, but they were just loafing around. As I looked down the street, they were loafing there also. Three men, as we were standing in front of the car, came across the street. They said to this man that was with me, "They want to see you inside." This man said to me, "I'll be right back." As he walked away from the car, and walked to go into this house, one of the men of the three said to me, "You better leave, because trouble is on the way." I looked at them, and let me tell you today, you ought to have the gift of discernment. If God is speaking to you, even through a child, you ought to be able to hear that. You ought not to be so blind, or your ears ought to not be so plugged that you don't hear the truth. When these three men said this to me, I felt an urgency that I better get out of there. They walked away and walked into the house with this other man. I said to myself, I better leave.

I went through a yard just adjacent to where the car was, and I began to see these ones that were loafing around. "What are you saying, Brother Pastor?" I'm saying that there are many

Christians today that are loafing around. There are many people today that are loafing around. Many Christians today are loafing around. As I walked in the yard and began to kind of walk away, I walked down through an alley, and I saw a motorcycle coming down the alley. Something said, "You better hide because it's getting dark." Before the person on the motorcycle could get up to me, he backed the motorcycle into the yard. Something said, "You better find another place to hide." I went over to a bush and stood there, kind of hiding a little bit, and then I saw a car coming down this alley. When it came down the alley, something said, "You better go and hide, because when the lights reflect off you, they'll be able to see you." I went adjacent to where I was and there was a rock there. I began to crouch down behind these bushes. As this car pulled up, it stopped in this drive by the bushes, and the lights went out. As I looked into the car, I saw an old man there. This old man, as he was gathering his stuff, and beginning to get out of the car, he leaned over. As I looked into his windows from this bush, I saw a huge cross on his neck. When I saw this cross, I knew help was there. I felt secure because the cross was there. I felt that everything was going to be alright because the cross was there. There's something about the cross of Jesus, something about God, when you have the blood of Jesus over you. You know that everything is all right.

Oh, the Lord is dealing with me today. I didn't know why I had that dream, but I sure know why I had it now. The Lord was telling me that I better be careful. The Lord was telling me that I better watch where I go. I better be careful where I stand. And I better do what the Lord says do. I don't know about you today, but God does reveal to us in dreams and in visions. We're living in an hour now, that a lot of things are going on. We better be careful, because the devil is out to get us any way that he can. He's out to trick us any way that he can. (Oh, help me today, Lord. Oh, Jesus, help me today, to understand what You're saying.) I'm mindful today, and I'm praying and I'm asking the Lord today, that wherever those ones are that are not doing the will of God, I want to get away from them. I want to stay away from them. I don't want to be bothered with them because I know what can happen to me.

God is saying that there are a lot of people that are not doing anything, but we are to stay away from them. We are to leave them alone. Oh, I'm glad today, not only was this for you, but it was definitely for me. (Oh, Lord, help me today, to stay away from them! -- oh, glory to God -- so I can do the work that You've called me to do! Oh, Lord, help me to keep my hands in Your hands so I can know everything will be alright.)

As I move on here today, I pray that you've gotten something from that dream or vision God gave to me. I know I have! And I tell you, I'm going to do something about it! Let me tell you today, Christ shows himself well-pleased with Peter's confession, for He said it was so clear and explicit. Christ shows him from whence he received the knowledge of the truth. For Jesus said to Peter in those verses that we read this morning, "Peter, I give unto thee the keys of things on heaven, and I give to thee the keys to things on earth. And whatsoever you shall bind on earth shall be bound in heaven, and whatsoever you loose on earth shall be loosed in heaven." Oh, I'm glad this morning that Jesus gave me a prescription today. I'm glad this morning that God is trying to get our attention.

Let me tell you this morning, if you will take a thought today that you can carry home with you, that is, "God always has a way out." I don't know about you this morning, but as I had that dream on the other day, the Spirit dealt with me and said "God has a way out." Don't you worry about what's going on: God has a way out. He is a way-maker, and that was the other part of that: Don't you worry, God is a way-maker. Oh, I'm glad today! He made a way for Abraham. Oh, glory to God! In Sodom and Gomorrah, He made a way for Lot! Oh, I'm glad today! He made a way for David when Saul was out to kill him. God made a way for him! God made a way - oh, glory to God! - for Jesus - oh, bless His name - when Jesus gave His life that we might have life! God is a way-maker! Oh, bless His name today! God is! He always has a way out! Oh, I'm glad today! The way may not be the way I want it to be, but God has a way out! It may not be the way you think it ought to be, but God has a way out! Oh, I'm glad this morning! As I saw that dream, the way out was a cross! The way out was the blood of Jesus! I want to tell you today, you better get close to somebody that knows the Lord! You better get close to somebody that can get a prayer through! You better get close to somebody that loves Jesus! Oh, I'm glad today! As I looked out over that rock that I was standing on, I saw the cross on the man's neck. I knew that everything would be alright. I want to tell you this morning, God is a way-maker! You can stand on His Word today! I'm glad! I'm glad!

I'm glad I'm standing, not on Peter this morning, but I'm standing the confession of Peter, when he said, "Thou art the Christ, the Son of the living God." I'm glad today! I'm glad today! I don't have to follow the traditions of men, but I can stand on the Word, the Word of God! Oh, bless His name today! God is a way-maker! You can stand on His Word today! I'm glad today! I'm not just preaching to you today, but it's a Word for myself! I'm glad today! My God is able today! Look at Jesus, the mighty Lamb of God! I wish today that I could go into the prisons this morning. I would tell them that God is way-maker! I wish I could go into the nursing homes! I would tell them this morning God is a way-maker! Oh, glory to God! I wish I could go where the crack smokers are. I would tell them this morning, "God is a way-maker!"

When many today are going about their own way, they're not concerned about the Lord or His work. They're not concerned about anybody. I would tell them today, my God today is a way-maker! I'm glad today; I can call on Him! I can call on Him! Oh, bless His name! I'm calling on Him right now! Jesus! The Christ! The Son of the living God! Jesus, my all in all. I want to tell you today, many people today don't care anything about the Word of God! If you're singing over here, they'll come in. If they're letting other things go on, they'll come in. But it's something about the Word of God! I love the Word of God! It's the only thing that will stand. I can tell broken homes, "God is a way-maker!" You can stand on His Word!

If I could testify for a little while, I remember a few years ago, before I accepted my calling in the ministry. I went to my pastor. I said, "Pastor, I feel the Lord wants me to preach His Word." My pastor said, "Are you sure?" Oh, glory to God! Let me tell you what I told him. I said, "Pastor, I'm sure." A couple weeks later I was at the church and my pastor said, "Pride, are you sure?" I said, "Oh, Pastor, I'm sure." Oh, glory! Oh, help me today! But let me tell you, the third time, a couple weeks later, the pastor said, "Are you sure that God has called you to preach His Word?" I got disturbed. I said, "Why does he keep asking me, am I sure? Why does he keep asking me if the Lord had called me to preach His Word?" I know now! You better be sure, if you're doing a work for the Lord, because the devil will always try to come against you! Oh, glory to God!

If you'll be patient with me today, I just want to testify. I went to my wife, I said, "Honey, the Lord has called me. You know I'm on the deacon board. You know I'm working with the trustees. You know I'm doing all kinds of things. I feel the Lord wants me to preach." She said, "If you preach, I'm going to divorce you. If you preach, I'm going to take the kids from you. If you preach, I'm going to take the house from you. If you preach, I don't want any part of it." Oh, glory! God is a way-maker! Let me tell you, I got on my knees, and I began to pray and talk with the Lord. I said, "Jesus, You're a way-maker. And I know that You are. You've brought me, Lord, from a mighty long way." Let me tell you, she went on her way. But I've been climbing God's way, sometimes up and sometimes down, and sometimes all around, even in circles. But God is a way-maker today! You can stand on His Word!

Here we are today, almost twenty years later, God is the same yesterday and forever. I'm glad today! And here I go again, I've got another situation! God is a way-maker! I'm going on with the Lord! I want to tell you today, I talked with the Father last night; not with Willie Pride, Sr., but with my Father in heaven. I told Him, "Lord, I don't understand, and I need your help, Jesus, all the way, all the way!" A man saw me looking up in the sky. I don't know what he saw in me, but when I got done talking, he came to me. He said, "I love to see a man that meditates. I love to see a man that looks up in the sky. I love to see a man whose got his mind made up." And I told the man, "I was talking, not with the stars, but I was talking with my Father. My Father, who is in heaven."

I know what Jesus meant - oh, bless His name today - I know what Jesus meant, when He went back, all the way! One of these days, we're going to go back to be with the Father! One of these days, we're going to go home to be with Him! One of these days - oh, glory to God - we're going to have to stack up our hymnals and Bibles and go on to be with Him. God is a way-maker today! Let me tell you today, you may not understand it, and neither do I, but God is a way-maker, oh, yes, He is! I'm trying to close here, but let me tell today, man didn't call you - oh, glory to God - and woman didn't call you. You ought to be so wrapped up in the Lord, tied up and tangled up that nobody can take away your joy! Nobody can take away what the Lord has called you to do! I'm glad today! He's a way-maker! Oh, bless His name! I'm glad today! Will you stand on His Word? Oh, bless His name! Not man's word, but the Word of God! I'm glad today! I'm standing on the Word! I'm glad today, for Jesus, the mighty Lamb of God.

I want to encourage you this morning, go on with the Lord! Keep your hand in God's hands! Everything, everything, everything! will be alright! I feel it now! I feel the angels, they're rejoicing right now! Why are they rejoicing? Because we're talking about Jesus! Jesus, the mighty Lamb of God! Look what He did! They hanged Him high on that tree, blood running down from His hands and His feet! My God is a way-maker today! Look at Jesus, hanging there, oh, bless His name! I can see Jesus! Oh, help me today! Oh, glory, oh glory! It's something about wanting to go home! Somebody said a couple weeks ago, "I wish the Lord would come right now." I know sometimes your burdens can get heavy, and you want to get out of here right now. But let me tell you, we've got a job to do! We've got a responsibility to the Lord!

And Jesus had a responsibility to die for sinners like you and me. Oh, Lord, oh, Lord! Thank You, Jesus, for dying on the cross. Thank You, Jesus, for hanging there, blood running down from Your hands and Your feet. But You didn't say a mumbling word, but, "Father, oh, my Father!" I feel my help now! Oh, bless His name! Thank You, Lord, that man didn't call me! Thank You, Lord, for the pastor that said, "Did God call you out?" He called me out, and He gave me what I needed! He wasn't short in His Word! He's never short when He deals with the saints of God! Oh, look at Jesus, dying there, oh, glory! But He didn't say a mumbling Word, but, "Father, oh, Father!" God is a way-maker today! You can stand on His Word! Oh, bless His name! Look at Jesus! They took Him down off that tree. Oh, bless His name! I'm glad today, oh, bless His name, you're not following me, but you're following the Lord! Oh, bless His name! When you follow Jesus, He'll never lead you wrong, He'll never lead you astray! When you're following Jesus, He'll pick you up when you're down! He'll turn your feet all the way around. He'll place them on a solid rock. They took Him off that tree, they placed Him in borrowed tomb, all day Saturday, oh bless His name! Somebody said - oh, glory to God! - He had to die, He had to lay there, all day Saturday - oh, glory to God! - all night Saturday night - oh, bless His name! I can see Jesus talking to some of the older prophets, telling them, "I'm here with you, only for a little while, but I've got to get up so you can get up one day, on that resurrection day." But early Sunday morning, look at the angels, they came down, they rolled the stone away! Oh, glory! Man didn't do it! Oh, Mary and Martha didn't do it! But the angels rolled the stone away! When they rolled it away, oh, glory, I see Jesus! Oh, bless His name today! I feel it now! I see Jesus, oh, glory, taking off his garment, taking off His burial clothes! I see Him taking it off! Oh, bless His name! Oh, I see Him sitting up - oh, glory to God - sitting up, and I see Him getting up, getting up on His feet, saying, "All power, all power, all power is in My hands!" I'm glad today! I'm glad today! "All power," He said, "is in My hands!"

I don't care what the world has to do; all power is in the hands of God! God is a way-maker today! We can stand on His Word! Oh, bless His name! And look at Jesus! Oh, glory to God! Getting on that cloud! Why would You leave me, Lord? You know what I'm going through, why would You leave me, Lord, all by myself? I hear Brother Peter saying, "Why would You leave me, Lord? Why would You leave me all by myself? I've been with You, Lord, I gave all I could give. I gave my money, I gave my time, Lord. I left my fishing boats. I left everything to follow You, Lord. Why would You leave me now?" I don't know about you today. Maybe you've never been in a position where you felt the Lord left you. But let me tell you today, Jesus said, "If I don't go," -- oh, bless His name! -- "It won't come." Thank God, I'm filled today! Not filled with some garbage, not filled with wine from the liquor store, but thank God, I'm filled with the new wine!

What is that new wine that will fill you up? What is that new wine, when you almost have an accident and you don't cuss anybody out? What is that new wine, when they try to gossip at you and you don't want to hear it? What is that new wine, knowing that you need a blessing, and knowing that it only comes from God! What is that new wine? Oh, God is a way-maker today! Oh, help me today, Lord! I feel like stepping out on His Word, which I am. But God is a way-maker! Look at Jesus, oh, glory, getting on that cloud, going all the way back, all the way to glory! I don't know about you today, if you've ever felt so all alone, but let me tell you, you don't have to be. Jesus said, "I send you Something! Holy Ghost power! I send you Something, when things aren't right, it'll change your attitude and make it right!"

I'm glad today, Jesus sent the Holy Ghost! He sent it down, all the way from heaven. Why do you think today that Christians act the way they act? They don't have any power. They don't have any power! But let me tell you today, as I close here, God is a way-maker! Is He a way-maker for you? Oh, bless His name today! Is He a way-maker? Oh, yes, He is! I know He's a way-maker! I can lift both hands to Him! Thank You, Lord, oh, thank You, Lord! As I close here this morning, God is, oh, God is! everything that you need! Don't you worry about what the world says! Don't you worry about the tricks of the devil. God is a way maker! Thank You, Lord, oh, thank You, Lord, for what You're doing right now.

As I close today, we need that power, that wonder-working power. I thank You, Lord! Oh, glory to God. Somebody said, "It's like fire shut up in my bones!" Fire! Oh, glory to God! It wakes me up in the morning with a song in my heart! I used to wake up and run to the coffee pot! I used to wake up and run to the bathroom! But when I wake up now, I wake up and go down on my knees! Thank You, Lord, oh, Lord, thank You, Jesus, for what You're doing right now! I'm glad today for who the Lord is! Oh, glory to His name! Thank You, Lord. God is a way-maker. Hallelujah today! He's a way-maker. He's a burden-bearer, oh, bless His name. I'm so glad Jesus lifted me!

If you don't have any power, you can come now. Come to Jesus, just as you are.

THE DIVINE SEARCH
John 4:23-26

Turn with me today to the book of St. John, the 4th chapter, where our Scripture reading is coming from, beginning at the 23rd verse.

23. But the hour cometh, and now is, when the true worshippers shall worship the Father in spirit and in truth: for the Father seeketh such to worship him.
24. God is a Spirit: and they that worship him must worship him in spirit and in truth.
25. The woman saith unto him, I know that Messias cometh, which is called Christ: when he is come, he will tell us all things.
26. Jesus saith unto her, I that speak unto thee am he.

From that 23rd verse this morning, I want to take a thought of the subject today, that you might carry home with you, "The Divine Search."

When the wise men came to find the baby Jesus, they came to worship Him. My question this morning to you, do you come to worship Him? Not 'him' pointing to myself' but Him, Jesus, the Christ, the Son of God? Or do you come to find fault? Or do you come to gossip? Or do you come not to conform with the Word of God?

The wise men had their minds open, because when they went to search for the Child, they went with the spirit of worship within themselves. You might say this morning, "Why is the church building not full? Where is Brother and Sister what's-their-name?" But unless you come with the spirit of worship, you're not going to receive anything. If you come to the house of God for the show, then you're not going to receive anything. You should always come to the house of God, not only to just receive, but to give blessings as well. I'm not knocking church-goers, but I'm simply saying there are church buildings this morning filled to capacity with the show, some wearing fancy hats, some wearing the Botany 500 suits, and some wearing expensive dresses. Everybody is looking at everybody else, seeing what they look like, what they smell like, and what their physical condition might be.

But I want to tell you that the Divine Search is the search of worshiping Jesus in spirit and in truth. The wise men came to worship Jesus. We can see from the text today, 'that the hour cometh, and now is, when true worshipers come to worship the Father in spirit and in truth: for the Father seeketh such to worship Him.'

We're grateful to God today that we can lift up His holy name. We can worship Him because He is worthy to be praised. We can lift Him up today, because He gives us a joy that the world didn't give and the world can't take away. The Scriptures tell us that we should seek God. This is naturally impossible. You would think, this morning, that everybody who passes these doors, going up and down the streets should see it naturally so, to worship and seek the Lord.

But I'm going to tell you this morning, there are millions and millions who are not seeking God. Let me tell you today, God is sitting high and looking low. He's calling the roll. Every time you pick up your newspaper, you hear about devastation on every hand. Every time you talk to your neighbor he's saying, "Did you know that person was killed, and this person was this, and that person was that?" It seems like you never hear news of good times. But I want to tell you today, that true worshipers must worship Him in spirit and in truth.

A sister just a couple of days ago told me, "We go to St. James Church." I said, "That's all right, but you're invited to come worship with us." "Oh," she said, "I was just visiting." And I said, "Praise the Lord." The true worshipers on the divine search have a relationship with God like no one else.

As we see this morning from our text today, there are two things that the true worshiper must seek. Number one, he seeks the spiritual nature of the Subject of his quest. Number two, they who seek Him know they are His children. When we realize the Fatherhood of God, and that the life we're leading is eternal, the difficulty disappears. Then one can concern himself with such a quest as this.

We can see that true worshipers on this divine search must worship Him in spirit and in truth. God is the Father, not just of heaven, but He's the Father of this earth. When God seeks His true worshipers of His people, they are His children that the Father desires. We are to seek the Lord while He may be found.

We are to lift up His holy name. We are to know, without a doubt, in the midst of the storm, God truly is in control. But I want to leave this thought with you this morning: when you come to the Lord's house, you ought to always leave better than you were when you came.

I'm glad about that this morning, because there's something about the Word of God. There's something about knowing that I've heard a Word from the Lord. It's something about knowing that God's Word will wash me. It's something about knowing the God's Word will make me. It's something about God's Word that will build up my faith. And as I build up my faith, I will always know that God truly is in control. So, I'm glad this morning, we serve a God who has all power in His hands.

I want to tell you this morning, seek ye the Lord while He may be found. "What are you saying, Pastor?" I'm saying that one of these days you're going to come looking for the church, and the church is going to be gone. You're going to be looking for those ones that have been baptized and filled with the Holy Ghost and fire, and they're going to be gone. "What are you saying, Pastor?" I'm saying that Jesus is coming and He's calling for people that have been washed in the blood of the Lamb. He's calling for a people, -- praise His holy name, -- who know Him, who worship Him in spirit and in truth. God seeks true worshipers by manifesting Himself. God is calling people who love Him, who have been washed in the blood of the Lamb.

I have to testify here today. Just the other day, I was down at the courthouse. There was this man sitting there as I went in, and as I came out of court. Let me you, everybody, believe me, they know what their condition is. If it's a sin-sick soul, they know what their condition is. If it's a backsliding state, they know what their condition is. Whenever it is, they know what their condition is. And this man said to me, "I know I'm not doing what I should be doing." And he said to me, "I know that I'm lacking in faith." And the man went on to say, "When I try to do good, my so-called friends, they make me do things I don't want to do." That said something to me. Many of our loved ones are doing things they don't want to do. We've tried to tell them that Jesus is the answer.

One day we'll stand before the judgment seat of Christ. You might say this morning, "Oh, Pastor, it seems like everybody is getting away with something." Let me tell you this morning, nobody is getting away with anything. My God has got a record keeper. Oh, bless His name. It'll never burn out. My God, today, knows what is going on in the world. He made it. He knows all about it. The Lord is a way-maker. The Lord is a burden-bearer. I'm glad today. I don't need 10,000 to say a word for Jesus. All I need is the spirit of true worship. You ought to, my sisters and brothers, tell somebody, everywhere you go, "I know the Lord has been good. He's been good to me." Everywhere you go, you ought to have a testimony about Jesus, the mighty Lamb of God, Mary's baby. I'm so glad today, I'm a true worshiper of Jesus Christ. Everywhere I go, I can let my light shine. Everywhere I go, I can lift Him up. For He said in His Word, if He be lifted up, He will draw all men unto Him.

I'm glad this morning. I'm a true worshiper of Jesus Christ. As we look back at the sermon message this morning, by actual indication of His Word, His Word will never pass away. His Word will stand forever. If you are standing on the Word, if you're standing on the Word of God, no matter what others might say, you can stand. I'm glad I'm standing on the Word of God. Look at us today. We've been thankful all year, and we've grown all year long. Each of us is protected. We're better than we were last year, because of worshiping the Lord and lifting Him up and praising His name.

I'm glad this morning! Jesus is the mighty Lamb of God – I feel it now coming down from heaven – He is the mighty Lamb of God! Jesus, thank You for the Holy Ghost, Lord. Thank You for the moving of the Spirit of God. I'm glad! I'm glad! If the Lord comes right now, where would you go? Would you go to heaven to be with Jesus? Or would you go to hell to be with the devil? I want to go to be with the Lord. I want to walk the streets of gold. They're fighting down here for gold, but on the other side, we're going to walk the streets of gold. Thank You, Lord. No Dow Jones is going to dictate to us there. Nobody can dictate to us there. And, oh, glory, when we get there, I'm going to put on my wings. Somebody said, "I'm going to put on my wings and I'm going to fly all over God's heaven." Thank You, Jesus, for what You're doing right now.

On the divine search of the Most High, He will make everything all right. I'm glad! I'm glad this morning, I'm a worshiper of the Lord God, and Him only shall I serve. That says something. We're not just going to get over there and sit down, we're going to serve. We're going to serve the Lord Jesus; Jesus, my King; Jesus, Lord of all. Oh, thank you, Lord, for what You're doing right now. We're going to serve Him in the morning, serve Him at noonday, serve Him all night long.

You might ask this morning, "Why seek God?" Let me tell you why you ought to seek Him. You ought to seek Him to praise Him. It's something about the praise of God. It's something about lifting Him up. It's something about having a song down in your heart. Oh, glory to God. I've got a song. I don't know all the words to it, but every now and then when I want to get some extra joy, I think about that song down in my heart, and I begin to sing, and the wheels begin to turn on the inside. The wheel and the fire begin to burn. Sometimes I feel all by myself, but I think about Jesus, my All in all. The Divine Search this morning, if you came to praise the Lord, everybody ought to know you came to lift Him up. Look how many this morning came to Sunday school, and that was all right, but very few came for the Word. That's how the devil keeps you out of faith. Come in now, hear me, hear the Word of God. Why do you think the church is so weak today? They're not hearing a Word from a Lord. I'm glad! I'm glad! I hear a Word! I feel it now! Oh, glory to God. I feel it moving down on the inside. Oh, thank You, Lord.

Oh, bless His name. I'm going to be in revival this month and I'm revived already! I've got a Word from the Lord. Thank You, Jesus. Oh, bless His name! I'm going to Phoenix. Oh, glory to God! I'm going to Los Angeles. Oh, glory to God, a Word from my King. I'm glad! I'm glad! I'm glad today! I can feel something moving down in my heart. You ought to have something. It will make you want to move. It will make you want to shout. I'm thankful to the Lord; I've got a testimony. Oh, bless His name. The Lord of glory is good. The Lord, the Lord is good! Why don't you seek Him today?

You should tell somebody, "I know the Lord is good." This is not a good message for everybody to hear, because everybody doesn't want to worship the Lord. But if I didn't have any legs, I would just wave my hands and worship the Lord. If I didn't have any arms, I'd just move my head and worship the Lord. Oh, I worship Him today. He wants to be praised. Everywhere you go, you ought to tell somebody about Jesus, the One the who died for your sins, the One who gave His life for you and for me.

I love Him today more than I loved Him yesterday. It gets sweeter and sweeter as the days go by. (Thank You, Lord, for what You're doing right now.) Look at Jesus! Glory to God! Look at Jesus. Why seek God? Why seek Him? All worship should be evidence of the closeness, the accessibility of God. All worship should be a state of mind, that I know when I come to the House of God, I'm not only going to receive, but I'm going to give. Let me tell you this morning, as I move on here, the Lord is good! The Lord is good! As I read My Bible, as I hear the Word of the Lord, I know the Lord is good! You can stand today on the Word, the Word of God. Somebody told me, "I don't know the way." But let me tell you, Jesus is the Way. If you're not standing this morning, it's not because Jesus isn't able. You can stand on the Word of God.

Thank You, Jesus, for what You're doing right now. I'm glad, and I'm closing this morning. I'm glad that Jesus was hanging there on that cross, blood running down from His hands and from His feet, but He didn't say a mumbling word, but, "Father, My Father, forgive them for they don't know what they do." I'm glad today, for the mighty Lamb of God. I'm glad that Jesus, the mighty Lamb of God, is able to make a way out of no way. I'm glad this morning that my God is able today. I can put my trust, not in men, but I can put my trust in God. But look at Jesus, dying there, blood running down, they hanged Him, and they put a crown of thorns on His head. Oh, bless His holy name. He didn't say a mumbling word. I'm glad they pierced Him in the side. They tried Him and they condemned Him, but the Word of God had to be fulfilled. The Word of God has to come to pass. Oh, bless His name.

Let me ask you this morning, are you condemning Him right now? I don't want to condemn You, Lord, because I love You. I love You! I love You, Lord! I love You, Lord, down to my soul! Bless His name! Thank You, Jesus, for what You're doing right now.

They took Him down off that cross. Oh, glory to God. They placed Him in that tomb. They sealed it. I saw that when I went to Israel. They sealed it. They laid Him there. He lay there, in that tomb, all day Saturday. He lay there all night Saturday night, in that tomb. But Sunday morning, I see the angel coming down, coming down from heaven, and rolling the stone away. I see the angel rolling that big, old stone away. And I see Jesus in there. Oh, bless His name! Oh, glory to God! But God spoke, He spoke to Jesus. "Now get up. Get up, Son, be about Your Father's business." And I see Jesus, Jesus with His grave clothes on, getting up. Oh, bless God's name. I see Him as He shed the funeral clothes. I see Him taking off the funeral garment. And no sin in that body. Thank You, Lord! Thank You, Lord! And I can see Mary going down to the tomb, going down to worship the dead body there. When she went down, she saw angels.

"Who are you looking for, Mary?"

"I'm looking for Jesus."

"Let me tell you, Mary, He's not here, because He's risen from the grave, with all power in His hand."

I'm glad today! He got up, all power in His hand! Then He went all the way back to glory, and He sent the Holy Ghost that's within us, that leads us in the path of righteousness.

Let me tell you today, true seekers and worshipers of Jesus Christ can feel it down on the inside. Oh, bless His name. Did you hear me this morning? You know you ought to return to Him. Maybe you haven't accepted the Lord as your personal Savior. You need to come now. Somebody will say this morning, I came, and I was wounded and I was naked. I was lonely, and I was without, but I've found in Him a resting place. Let me tell you this morning, there's a resting place in Jesus. There's a resting place in Him. You can find a place in Him.

If you're here this morning, and you've never accepted the Lord as your personal Savior, you can come now. Oh, glory to God. Thank You, Lord. Are you here this morning? Can you hear the Word? Jesus said, "Harden not your heart." Oh, bless His name, because the Word of God is rich and it's good. Are you here this morning, out of a church home? God wants you to make this your church home. You need to come now. Come to Jesus. Come to Jesus.

FAITHFULNESS, FAILURE AND REPENTANCE
Mark 14:66-72

St. Mark, this morning, the 14th chapter, beginning at the 66th verse, reads to us today:

66. And as Peter was beneath in the palace, there cometh one of the maids of the high priest:
67. And when she saw Peter warming himself, she looked upon him, and said, And thou also wast with Jesus of Nazareth.
68. But he denied, saying, I know not, neither understand I what thou sayest. And he went out into the porch; and the cock crew.
69. And a maid saw him again, and began to say to them that stood by, This is one of them.
70. And he denied it again. And a little after, they that stood by said again to Peter, Surely thou art one of them: for thou art a Galilaean, and thy speech agreeth thereto.
71. But he began to curse and to swear, saying, I know not this man of whom ye speak.
72. And the second time the cock crew. And Peter called to mind the word that Jesus said unto him, Before the cock crow twice, thou shalt deny me thrice. And when he thought thereon, he wept.

I want to preach to you this morning from the thought of the subject from those few verses this morning, "Faithfulness, Failure and Repentance." Would you say that with me? "Faithfulness, failure, and repentance."

Here we see this morning, an account where Jesus had said to Peter, even before Jesus was crucified, that Peter would deny him, not one time, not two times, but three times. And do you not know the Bible says that the Word of God would bring all things to your remembrance? And here Peter was, denying the very idea that he was with Christ. Here Peter was, saying, "I don't even know the man you're talking about." Here Peter was, he had walked with Jesus. Here Peter was, one of the disciples that been three years with Jesus, but here he was, fearful, saying,

"I know not this man. I don't even know what you talk about." Judas betrayed Jesus and identified Him to the high priest, scribes and elders, and they arrested Jesus in the garden of Gethsemane. Using the only defense he knew, Peter cut off one of the Roman centurion's ear. When we criticize him so severely for denying Christ, we totally forget his courage. For he was the one who pulled out his sword, and he was the one who cut off the soldier's ear when they began to shift Jesus around. Rather than going on to the home of the high priest, where Jesus had been taken for a trial, Peter went hiding.

Let me tell you today, you may be able to hide from me, but you can't hide from God. I'm a living witness, there are many of us doing things that God is not pleased with. But let me tell you today, God will require us to give an account of those things. Peter's faithfulness to Jesus was unquestioned. He had promised the Lord, though all other may forsake Him, he would serve Him. That's when Jesus said, "Before the cock crows twice, you will deny me three times, Peter." Jesus knew what was going to happen. When the chief priests, scribes and elders came to arrest Jesus, after Judas had pointed Him out to them, Peter slashed off one of the high priest's servant's ear. He showed his denial in that he was not going to stand idly by and allow his Savior to be arrested by the mob. I want to say today, many of us do things in anger, but you ought to let the Lord fight your battles. You ought to let Him be the one who takes control of every situation.

We're talking this morning about faithfulness, failure, and repentance. As we move into the message this morning, we are going to break it down and show you what the cost is of being faithful. Somebody would say this morning, "Oh, Pastor, I'm only faithful on Sundays." But let me tell you this morning, you ought to be faithful every day. Somebody would say this morning, "Oh, I only do my Christian duties on Sunday." But let me tell you this morning, every second of the day, you ought to be doing your Christian duty. Someone said to me a few months ago, "Oh, I'm a religious person." But let me tell you this morning, there are millions of religious people all over this world. But there is a difference in being religious and being a Christian. I want to tell you today, when you put on the full armor, and you put on the cloak of Christ, you are a Christian every day.

Somebody said to me the other day, "God saved me." I said, "Praise the Lord! But did He save your pocketbook? Are you so stingy that you won't give anything to the work of God?" Let me tell you this morning, if you're saved, sanctified, and filled, you ought to be saved all over. Your tongue ought to be saved. Your ears ought to be saved. Your mind ought to be saved. Your heart ought to be fixed. The stony heart, God ought to take out and put in a heart of flesh. You might say this morning, "Oh, Pastor, that doesn't apply to me." But let me tell you today, we ought to be trying to make heaven our home. We ought to be striving every second of the day to meet Jesus. Let me tell you this morning, the way to destruction is a broad way. "What are you saying, Pastor?" I'm saying there are many today that are headed to hell. Oh, bless God's name! You might say this morning, "Oh, Pastor, that's hard to think, that a loving God like Jesus could have so many going to hell." It's not Jesus! We make our own choice! Oh, bless God's name! Nobody can put you into heaven or hell. But glory to God! We can stand up for righteousness! We can stand up for the blood-stained banner of Christ, everywhere we go! And when the Lord comes, He will reward us, according to our works, according to our deeds, according to His commandments.

Oh, I'm glad today! I'm glad for the testimony of Brother Peter. Oh, glory to God! For he failed in some areas -- oh bless His name! -- but, glory to God, he had a repenting spirit! Look at David. God said that David was a man after His own heart. Why was he that way? He was that way because when he would do wrong, he would get on his knees. He would say, "Oh, God, I'm sorry. Oh, God, I made a mistake, forgive me!" Do we have that spirit today? Have we lied about someone, and we have gone to God and said, "Oh, God, I'm sorry?" Have we done others wrong, and have we gone and said, "Oh, God, I'm sorry?"

I remember a few years ago, I was doing a revival, and usually in my revivals I do a 12:00 noonday lesson, then I preach each night. I was doing in that revival teaching a course called "Renewing Old Acquaintances." I was sharing with the people of that particular church that you ought to have a repenting spirit. If I've done somebody wrong, I ought to be able to go to God and go to that person and say, "I'm sorry." If you look at your church covenant on the wall over here, it clearly says that you must do that without delay. Because you don't know when the Lord might come. Someone said, "Don't let the sun go down on your wrath," which means if you lie down at night and you've got all of this on your shoulders, you could die in your sleep! You should not want to lie down that way! You should want to lie down and turn it over to the Lord, telling the Lord, "I want You to take control of it." Oh, bless His name today!

Oh, we're talking about this morning, faithfulness, failure, and repentance. Someone now decides to stir up the fire and add to it, to carry them through the night. The blaze shines upon Peter's face as he warms himself, and the high priest's servant girl recognizes him as being one of the disciples of Christ. As I said, you may hide from me, but you can't hide from God. In Mark 14:68, "And Peter denied him by saying, 'I neither know nor understand what you're talking about.'" This was his first denial, but he did not leave the courtyard, he just went out to the porch. I want to tell you this morning, you can't hide from God. Oh, bless His name today. I feel the Spirit coming on now. But let me tell you this morning, you ought to be able to take all your burdens to the Lord. Oh, I'm glad this morning for the testimony of Peter. I'm glad this morning that we can take our burdens, not to Peter, but we can take our burdens to the Lord. Oh, bless His name today! In this moment of human weakness, Peter has failed. This shows that even those who walk close to Christ are not unquestionably faithful and can experience weak periods and fail. They can be pressured from outside sources unexpectedly and fail. But let me tell you this morning, we don't have to fail. We have someone -- glory to God! -- who paid the price for all of our sins!

Oh, I'm glad this morning, as I move on here today, that I don't have to go to the priest this morning to tell him about what I did last night. I don't have to run to Everlasting and fall before the altar and try to get a prayer through of what I did yesterday. But I can go -- glory to God! -- to the Lord and tell the Lord all about it! Too many times, my sisters and my brothers, we want to go to everyone else with our problems, but let me tell you this morning, you ought to have a God, not a little bitty God, but a big God that's big enough to hear what you've got to say. I'm glad this morning for the faithfulness and for the failure of Peter.

It was an example to let us know that we, too, will fail, but glory to God! He will pick us up!

As I move on here, Peter immediately recognized his failure. After his third denial, the cock crowed, so it must have been around 3 A.M., the hour of the changing of the guards at the temple. When they changed, there was a bugle call that was called in the Latin language, "cock crow." Oh, I'm glad this morning for Jesus, the mighty Lamb of God! I'm glad this morning -- oh, bless His name today -- as I move on here, it looks like I'm moving too fast, but I'm trying to slow down.

Let me tell you this morning, you're not the keeper of yourself. You ought to be kept by the Spirit of God. This piercing sound rang out through the silent city and pierced the ears of Peter. As he remembered the words of Jesus, his heart was broken into a thousand pieces. Let me tell you this morning, you ought to have a love today, that the world didn't give and the world can't take away. You ought to have a joy today, regardless to what others might say, you ought to know you got it from the Lord. Oh, I'm glad this morning, only someone with great faithfulness could have been tempted so severely and failed, as Peter did, on that early morning in the courtyard in Jerusalem. As he remembered the words of Jesus, he also remembered the forgiveness of Jesus.

Let me tell you this morning, you can ask the Lord for forgiveness, no matter where you are. I'm glad! I'm glad! I'm glad I serve a God this morning that is not just in Michigan, where some of my folks are! I'm glad I serve a God this morning that's not just down South, where some of my family are. But I serve a God that's got all power in His hands! I don't know about you today! If you've ever been sick -- I don't mean just a headache, but I'm talking about sick in your body -- you've got a God today, you can go to -- oh, bless His name! -- He's got a line that's not like AT&T. I'm glad! I'm so glad! I can go to God in the midnight hour. I can go to God at noonday. I can go to God whatever the hour! I can tell Him all about my troubles. I can tell Him what I need. I don't know about you this morning. Maybe you've got a need in your life. Peter had a need in his life. Oh, Lord! You can go to God, oh, bless His name! and tell Him about all your problems.

Although Mark was a young man, he had observed many things about the disciples and their relationship with Jesus. This, Peter's own testimony, a firsthand account, would have left Christians of every age to know that though one fails, he does not have to fail. Christ is always willing -- oh, glory to God -- to forgive you this morning. Peter's forgiveness was far more effective than his failure was damaging. When he came aware of his failure, the Scripture says, he began to weep. It's something about weeping -- oh, glory to God -- I'm glad! I'm glad! It seems like every few months out of the year, I begin to weep. You might see me weeping sometime. I'm not weeping because I'm sad. I'm not weeping because I'm hurt. But I'm weeping because of the joy. You ought to shed a tear sometime. Something about a tear; the Lord will wipe the tears from your eyes.

I'm glad this morning for the testimony of Brother Peter. He began to weep, Mark 14:72. There's nothing more repenting than a teardrop. Some of you mothers know what I'm talking about. Oh, glory to God! Some of you fathers know what I'm talking about. There's nothing more repenting than a teardrop. Teardrops manifest the sincerity of the heart. The repentance of words can be merely exercise of the lips, but teardrops reach into the very depths of the pit of a broken heart. Teardrops express the confession of the heart and the soul for the misdeeds of the body. There's nothing upon this earth that is more revealing than a repentance teardrop.

Do you have some family members who don't know the Lord? I've got many today that are not saved. But I cry to the Lord, "Save them, Jesus!" I cry to the Lord, "Baptize them, Lord! and fill them up!" I believe today, if you who love the Lord would talk to God about your family, He will make a way for them. He'll turn your midnights into days! All you've got to do if you want your family saved, get on your knees and talk to the Lord. As I move on here, I didn't want to say all of that, but let me tell you this morning, we are not the keepers of ourselves.

As I move on here, a preacher was scheduled to preach at a church, and before he departed for his engagement, a registered letter arrived. The writer warned him not to come, threatening to tell the congregation publicly of an awful act of sin he had performed many years before. The minister proceeded with his plans to go on the way he was going. That Sunday morning, he was presented to preach, and before taking his text, he read the letter to the congregation, and he told them it was all true. The incident had occurred before he met the Lord. Let me put a note there. I don't know what you've done, I don't care what you've done, God is able -- oh, glory to God! -- to save your soul! God is able today to heal your body! God is able today to give you a mind stayed on Him. I can't believe I could sit in a church building for 40 or 50 years and live any kind of way. It's something about the Word of God. I believe the Lord and His Word! It's something about the Word, when you get it down on the inside! The prophet said, "It's like fire shut up in my bones!" I don't know about you today, but I love the Word of God! Oh, glory! I feel like preaching now! I wanted to cut off early, but let me tell you today, when you begin to work for the Lord, when you begin to step out on His Word, He will, He will make a way out of no way! I'm glad today! I love the Lord! Do you love my Jesus? Do you love Him? Oh, I love Him! Let me see your hands if you love my Jesus! Oh, Lord, I love Him today! Oh, bless His name!

As I move on here, the minister read the letter, but he had repented, and Christ had forgiven him. His life had been committed to serving Christ and preaching His Word. This congregation overwhelmingly accepted him. The message that Christ had sent him went on a little bit further. Only the faithful who have failed and have asked Christ to forgive them can bear the message of good news and glad tidings, and tell about a Savior who forgives failure and puts them on the right track. Sometimes the faithful, like the cars of an electric train, jump the track and turn over. If they're picked up, and put back on the track, they connect to the engine and they roll right along. I'm glad this morning, I can relate to that. If you're not on the track today, you can get on it right now. If you have not committed yourself to the Lord, you can do it right now. I'm glad today, for the Word of God!

Let me tell you today, as I move on here, it's something about the Word of God. You ought to take it and sanctify, down in your heart. I'm glad today! I'm glad today, for what Jesus did, the mighty Lamb of God. He died, that you might live. He gave His life, that you might have life! I'm glad this morning!

Oh, bless God's holy name! Look at Jesus hanging there, blood running down from His hands and His feet. But, oh, glory! He didn't say a mumbling word. There ought to come a time, you ought to not say anything. Just pray, oh, pray to the Lord. I'm glad today, I've got a prayer language. Somebody would say, "Is it in tongues?" Oh, it's not in tongues. I've got a prayer language, I can get on my knees and talk with my Father, even though He knows all in my heart.

I want to encourage you today, I want to encourage you, Jesus was hanging there on the cross, for your sins, for my sins. I'm glad this morning, they stretched Him wide! Oh, glory! Blood running down from His hands and His feet. But He didn't say a mumbling word, but, "Father, oh, Father!" Can you tell your Father you need Him today? My Father, who art in heaven! Oh, bless His name today! I want to encourage you this morning, stand on the Word, the Word of God! You can stand on the Word today! I'm glad! (I closed the door because that might have been the devil, trying to get in here at this time. It's something about the message of God, when the Word is going forth, and the invitation to Christ, the devil will always try to send a block. But let me tell you today, you ought to have a discernment. Oh, bless His name! You ought to have a discernment that you can call on the Lord. Call on Him today, oh, call on Him!)

As I close this morning, look at Jesus today! They took Him off that cross! Oh, bless His name! Oh, glory! They placed Him in a borrowed tomb. The Word says, all day Saturday, He laid there. Oh, bless His name! He laid there all day Saturday, oh, bless His name, all night Saturday night, but early, early Sunday morning, He got up! He got up with all power! All power was in His hands! You ought to have some get-up power. You ought to have some power when the devil comes against you. You ought to be able to stand. I'm glad today! I've got some power! "Where is it coming from, preacher? What kind of power do you have? Do you have electric power?" Oh, no, that's not what I'm talking about. What kind of power, when they lie upon you, you can go on with the Lord? What kind of power do you have when you're sick in you body, you can go on with the Lord? What kind of power do you have, when you don't have any money? What kind of power do you have, knowing that God will make a way for you? Let me tell you today, Holy Ghost Power! Jesus said, "If I don't go, it won't come." I'm glad today, it came down! It came down! It came down! It came down! I'm glad Jesus went all the way back, but He sent me some power! Oh, bless His name! Not white power, not black power, but Holy Ghost Power! Oh, bless His name! I'm glad this morning, for the mighty Lamb of God. Do you have some power today?

As I close this morning, look at Jesus, -- oh, bless His name! -- getting on that cloud, going all the way back, all the way to glory! If you're here this morning and you've got no power, maybe you've never accepted the Lord as your personal Savior. Let me tell you, nobody can do you like Jesus! Nobody! No wine store, no crack or cocaine. Nobody, not even your husband or your wife. Nobody can do you like the Lord. Oh, bless His name today. If you're here this morning and you've never been baptized, you've never accepted the Lord as your personal Savior, you can come now, just as you are. You don't have to get yourself ready. Somebody said on the other Sunday, "Wait until I quit smoking and quit lying." I said, "No! You'll never quit smoking, you'll never quit lying. But come as you are!" Oh, glory to God! I'm glad today, I came to Jesus as I was, wounded, naked and tired. But I found in Him, a resting place. And He has made me glad. If you're here this morning and you're out of a church home, and you've got no church home, and you feel the Lord wants you to be a part of this church family; somebody would say today, "Well, I'm out of a church, I don't have a home." Let me tell you this morning, Jesus said you have a home in Him.

If you're here this morning and you haven't accepted the Lord as your personal Savior, you can come now.

VICTORY IN CHRIST
I Corinthians 15:51-58

Truly today, we can take it to the Lord and leave it there, and believe me today, God knows and He cares. We ask ourselves a question today, "Is there a Word from the Lord?" I want to say this morning, there's always a Word from God. It may not come in the way that you feel it should come, but God always has a Word for us. He always has a Word for His people. We're grateful to God today for what He has done, and what He is doing, and what He's going to do, not only just here today, but what He's doing in our world right now.

If you would turn with me in your Bibles this morning, to the 15th chapter of First Corinthians, for there is a Word from the Lord today. We want to share with you this morning, so that your faith may be strengthened. The Bible says that faith cometh by hearing, and hearing by the Word of God. I'm a living witness today, the only way that your faith, my faith, any believer's faith can be strengthened, it has to be by the Word. Someone would say this morning, oh, it's the singing, oh, it's the testimonies, but no, it's not. It's the Word of God that strengthens your faith, my faith. It is the Word of God that strengthened the prophets' faith of old. As we read our Bibles, it says that Abraham's faith was strengthened because he believed God. When God spoke to him and told him to leave his family, and leave his kindred, it was faith that Abraham stepped out on. It was faith that told Moses to go back to Israel, and to tell Pharaoh to let God's people go. It was faith that Moses had to rely upon. It was faith that each of the prophets had to move in the realm of God, as God had directed.

It is faith today that is moving us. You may say this morning that you are moving on your own, but you aren't. You're moving because of God. He touched the button of nature this morning and woke you up. You didn't wake yourself up. Somebody would say this morning that it was the alarm clock. But it was God! Because I know this morning, that even the alarm going off, if God hadn't touched you, the alarm buzzing, or ringing or whatever, you would have slept right on, if God hadn't awakened you. I'm glad this morning for faith that we have, not in ourselves, but the faith we are to have in the Lord

Jesus Christ. We are grateful to God this morning for that faith on today.

As we look at chapter 15 of First Corinthians, the 51st verse, where our reading is coming from, verse 51 through verse 58, it reads to us:

> 51. Behold, I shew you a mystery; We shall not all sleep, but we shall all be changed,
> 52. In a moment, in the twinkling of an eye, at the last trump: for the trumpet shall sound, and the dead shall be raised incorruptible, and we shall be changed.
> 53. For this corruptible must put on incorruption, and this mortal must put on immortality.
> 54. So when this corruptible shall have put on incorruption, and this mortal shall have put on immortality, then shall be brought to pass the saying that is written, Death is swallowed up in victory.
> 55. O death, where is thy sting? O grave, where is thy victory?
> 56. The sting of death is sin; and the strength of sin is the law.
> 57. But thanks be to God, which giveth us the victory through our Lord Jesus Christ.
> 58. Therefore, my beloved brethren, be ye stedfast, unmoveable, always abounding in the work of the Lord, forasmuch as ye know that your labour is not in vain in the Lord.

Let us pray.

Our Father and our God, we thank You now, for what You've done, and what You're going to do. For You said in Your Word that heaven and earth would pass away, but Your Word would stand forever. Oh, heavenly Father, we pray You'd use these lips of clay, not my will, but Thy will be done. Oh, heavenly Father, open up our blind eyes today, that we might be not just a hearer of Your Word, but a doer of Your Word, for You said in Your Word that our works would not be in vain. Oh, heavenly Father, we praise You today, we praise You for this place of worship, that we can come together and praise Thy holy name. For You said if You be lifted up, You would draw all men. Lord God, we pray that the Spirit of God would go from beyond these four walls, go out into the hedges and highways, lift up bowed down heads, where ones are complacent today. Lord God, stop that complacency and let them know that we need to be about our Father's business. Thank You, Lord Jesus, for what You've done. Thank You for the power of the Holy Ghost, that You said would lead us and guide us into all truth and righteousness. Thank You, Lord Jesus, that we can stand on Your Word today. Now, Lord, stop by here with the presence and power of Your Holy Spirit. In Jesus' name we pray, thank You, Lord, thank You, Lord, thank You, Lord. Amen, amen and amen.

I was asked the other day what I thought heaven would be like. Let me tell you, sisters and brothers, there are many today who are confused about heaven. We have a misconception, as Christians, of what heaven is. A lot of us seem to think that when we get to heaven, we're going to start loving there. A lot of us seem to think that when we get to heaven, we're going to start giving there. A lot of us seem to think that when we get to heaven we're going to have everything straightened out. But let me tell you this morning, this that we're in, this earth, this physical body that we're in right now, this is the preparation ground.

Somebody said a few months ago, that we're in the land of the living, getting ready for the land of the dying. I say, 'oh, no,' to that. For we're in the land of the dying, getting ready for the land of the living. Oh, I feel like preaching this morning. For I know that heaven is a real place. I know that heaven is a place where I'm going to see my great-grandmother there. Heaven is a place where I'm going to see my father there. Heaven is a place where I'm going to see Dr. Abernathy there. Heaven is a place where I'm going to see my sister, Gertrude, there. Heaven is a place where I'm going to see Abraham, Isaac and Jacob there. Heaven is a place where I'm going to see Moses there. Oh, let me tell you this morning, the Bible says that heaven is a place where Jesus said that He would go away to prepare for us, a place where Jesus said, "In my Father's house there are many mansions." And Jesus said, "If it were not so, I would have told you." I'm glad this morning, for heaven today. Somebody would say this morning, "Are you trying to hurry to make it to heaven?" No, I'm not, but I want to be there! Oh, bless the name of the Lord! I want to be there when the Lord says, "Good and faithful servant, come on up a little bit higher! Come on up and be with me! Come on up!" Oh, bless the Lord's holy name!

Somebody asked me the other day, what will heaven be like? We were walking on some real nice carpet when he asked me that. I said, "We're walking on a beautiful carpet today, but when we get to heaven, we're going to walk the streets of gold." We're going to walk the streets of gold! I'm glad this morning that God will be our light! No more light bills on the other side! I'm glad this morning that we're going to have a light on the other side, and that light will be God! I'm glad this morning. The Word says in Revelation that there's going to be a tree, and that tree is going to have leaves on it, and the Word says that whenever you get sick, you can go to that tree - oh, bless God's name! - and break off a little branch, or a little leaf, and in that leaf, there's enough medicine in it to heal a nation. I'm glad! No headaches on the other side! No more goodbyes on the other side! I'm moving fast here! I haven't even gotten to what my text is this morning, but it's something about heaven that stirs me up. Oh, Lord! It's something about knowing that this is not my home, but I'm just a traveler passing through! I'm glad!

I'm glad this morning, that I have victory, and that is what I want to preach about this morning. I want to preach about victory! Not victory with the M-1 machine gun, not victory according to what man says is victory, but victory in Jesus! Oh, bless His name today! I'm glad! I'm glad this morning. Paul tells them that all the saints would not die, but all will be changed, from corruption to incorruption. What does that say to you? It says that these bodies are going back to the dust. I don't care what kind of physical shape you may think you might be in, these bodies are going back to the dust.

I'm mindful, just a week or so ago, one of the airlines persons was telling me that they had a situation where they had two men who had died, and they were coming from Minneapolis. One body was going to someplace in New York, and one body was going to Los Angeles. They transport bodies just like they used to do years ago on the train, but now they transport them on airplanes. The agent was telling me, they had two bodies, and when they got to Los Angeles, one body went on to New York, where it was supposed to go, and the other one stayed in Los Angeles, where it was going to be cremated. The one that was going to be cremated was an A.I.D.S. carrier. Let me tell you, when the remains got to New York City, the undertaker opened up the casket, with the family there, and they had the wrong body inside the casket. The one that was supposed to have been going there had been cremated already in Los Angeles. But let me tell you, as I thought about that, my Bible says, these bodies are going to have to go back to the dust. They're going to be changed! Oh, bless God's holy name! In the moment, in the twinkling of an eye! Let me tell you this morning, regardless to what man does to your body, my God has got your spirit, home to be with Him! Victory today, in the Lord! Oh, bless His name today!

As I move on here, because flesh and blood cannot inherit the kingdom of God, the apostle here makes known a truth unknown before, which is that the saints living at the Lord's second coming will not die. Do you not know, sisters and brothers, you don't have to die! "What do you mean, Brother Pastor?" Jesus has already come. He came as a babe in Bethlehem. Jesus has already died on the cross, and He's coming back. Do you not know, the Word of God is being fulfilled so very fast? And let me tell you today, He could come right at this hour, and we would meet Him in the clouds. We wouldn't have to die! We wouldn't have to go through all the things that some are going through in the hospital this morning. We wouldn't have to go through being killed by a drunk driving an automobile. We wouldn't have to die of some other disease of the body, but if Jesus came right now, we would go home, to be with Him. I'm glad this morning! We don't have to die, because the Lord is coming back, and He could come right now. The Word says we'll be changed in the moment, in the twinkling of an eye. And at the sound of the last trump - oh, bless His name today - at this summons, the graves shall open, and the dead saints shall rise incorruptible. The living saints will be changed into the same incorruptible state.

I'm glad this morning! We ought to have victory today! Not victory in ourselves, but it ought to be victory in the Lord. I'm glad this morning, regardless to what's going on, regarding this change. The Word says the reason for this change, the corruptible body must be made incorruptible, and this mortal body must be changed into immortality. Oh, bless His name today! What is sown must be quickened. I'm glad this morning for the Spirit of God! It's sown in my heart! Victory today, in the Lord! Victory today, in Jesus! What will follow this change of the living and the dead in Christ? The Word says, "Then shall be brought to pass the saying that says, Death is swallowed up in victory." I'm glad this morning! Christ hinders it from swallowing up His saints when they die. When they rise again, death shall be swallowed up forever, when we rise to meet Him in the clouds. Victory, in His name! I'm glad today, I've got victory in the name of the Lord! You've got victory in the name, the name of Jesus, the name above every name! I dare you this morning to apply that name to any situation. I dare you this morning, whatever it is, just say, "Jesus, my all in all, Jesus, my Lily of the valley, Jesus, my bright and morning Star!" I'm glad this morning - oh, bless His name today - I have victory in the Lord.

We fear no further because of the mysteries from these, but deny the power of the grave, for Jesus said, "I have the keys, not only to heaven, but I have the keys to hell." Let me tell you this morning, we have the victory, for the prison doors are burst open, and we are forever released.

I'm glad this morning, for the mighty Lamb of God. As I move on here today, I want to tell you today, we can stand on the Word. The victory the saints obtain is only through the Lord Jesus Christ. There is no other way you have victory than through the Lord. I want to tell you this morning, you ought to have some get-up power, knowing that Jesus has given you a joy that the world didn't give - oh, bless His name - and the world can't take away. You ought to have a resurrection, down on the inside! When trouble comes your way, you ought to have something to say, like Job said, "Though You slay me, Lord, yet will I serve You. I'm not going to turn my back on You, but I'm going to believe, and stand on Your Word." I'm glad this morning!

It seems like today, the church is growing cold. But let me tell you this morning, we have a victory that's not in the Baptist Church, but we have a victory in the Lord! I say to you this morning, put your hand in God's hand, and everything will be alright! I'm glad! I'm so glad today! I can move in the Spirit of God. I can say, "Lord, have Your way! Have your way, Lord

God, in every situation!" Oh, glory to God! Thank You, Lord, for giving me time. I can take the watch off now! Oh, bless His name! I'm glad this morning! I can stand on His Word! Let me tell you this morning, this is victory that overcometh the world, even our faith. Who then is born again is born of God, for which is the result of the regeneration and consequently for the other world. We are born when we are born in the Spirit of God. He prepares us for the other side. I'm glad this morning! I say this morning, you have the victory in the name of the Lord! The name of Jesus - oh, glory to God! - is above every name!

As I move on here this morning, they shall eat of the tree of life which is in the midst of paradise, not in the earthly paradise, but the heavenly paradise. Be now faithful unto death, and the Word says, "I will give you a crown of life. I'll give you a crown. I'll reward you. I'll reward you openly, and I'll reward you in other ways. A crown of life to reward those who are faithful even unto death." Let me tell you this morning, I don't care who goes on, you ought to go on with the Lord. Let nobody get in your way of serving your God. He's good! He's good today! He's better than that! He's very good! Oh, bless His name today! He woke us up early this morning! He started us on our way! Oh, bless His name today!

The purity of grace shall be rewarded with the perfect purity of God's glory. Holiness, when perfected, shall be its own reward. Glory is the preparation of grace. And this is why you hear me say, "Glory Hallelujah!" You ought to say, "Glory Hallelujah!" to Jesus, your King, the Lord of lords, my all in all! I'm glad this morning! You ought to have a glory this morning that the world didn't give and the world can't take away. Here we are, celebrating communion Sunday, the first Sunday of the new month. You ought to have a glory of knowing that Jesus said, "Partake of My body, and partake of My blood. As often as you do this, you do this in remembrance of My death, burial and resurrection." I'm glad today! We have the victory, not in man, but we have the victory in the Lord! Thank You, Lord! Whatever it is, victory rewards the promises made to the overcoming believer. It was now possible that by the reproofs and counsels of Christ that we might be inspired with fresh zeal and fervor. You ought to have a zeal for God. You ought to have a love for the Lord! Oh, bless His name today! You ought to have a love that you've got Him down in your soul. I'm glad this morning! I'm glad today, that I have victory in the Lord!

As I move on here this morning, the day breaks and the shadows flee away. A new world now appears, the former having passed away. The things of the world ought to pass away. You ought to have a conversation about the Lord. Too many Christians today talk about too much other stuff, instead of talking about the things of God. Let me tell you this morning, if you put your mind on Him, He'll make a way. He'll turn your midnights into day. Isaiah said, "He will give you perfect peace, whose mind is stayed on Him." Let me tell you this morning, you ought to have your mind stayed on the Lord! Your mind ought to be on Him, every second of the day! It ought to be on the Lord. I'm glad this morning! I've got a mind today -- oh, glory to God! -- to run on for Him! I might get tired sometimes, but there's a song, "I've been running for Jesus a long time, and I'm not tired yet." Have you been running for Him a long time? Your body gets tired, but your Spirit shouldn't get tired. You ought to run on for the Lord and not get tired.

There shall be neither death, nor pain, and therefore no sorrow, no crying there. The former things have passed away. But it should be consistent with the goodness of God and His love for His people, to create in them a holy desire to worship Him in all their ways. A holy desire to stand upon the Word of God, and they will divide them their proper sanctification, and therefore they may be assured that He will give them the foundation of the water of life freely. Let me tell you this morning, do you have the water of life? Oh, bless His name! Is it freely flowing outside of you? Is it freely flowing inside of you? I'm glad this morning! Jesus said, "If I don't go, It won't come!" I'm glad this morning - oh, bless His name today! - for the mighty Lamb of God.

Let me tell you this morning, we have the victory in the name of the Lord. We have the victory, not in my father's name, but in the name of Jesus. You have the victory this morning! I don't care what the condition may be! You have the victory in the name of the Lord. I'm glad this morning. I can claim the promises of God's Word - oh, bless His name - and by His stripes, we are healed today! Not that the medicine can't do you some good, because it can, but you ought to be healed by His stripes, the stripes that He bore on Calvary's cross. I'm glad! I'm glad today! I can stand on His Word! I'm glad today, that nobody can do me like Jesus! Nobody can do me like the Lord. I'm glad today. You ought to have the victory in every situation.

Let me move on here this morning. We have the victory, not in man, but in the Lord. I want to tell you this morning, you might say, "I'm sick, I'm sick in my body, and I'm sick in my sin." But this is the hospital! Right here where you are, this is the hospital! You can be healed today! You can be delivered today! Your eyes can be opened today! Your mind can be regulated today! This is a hospital! Oh, bless His name today! Many people today are trying to find the answers in sociology, or trying to find the answers in psychology, or trying to find the answers in a lot of these other programs. But let me tell you today, the only answer is in the Lord! The only answer is in the Lord! Let me say that again! Victory in His name today! I've got a friend that's going to Schick this next week to try to get over his situation. I told him a couple weeks ago, we've got the answer. I said, "Brother, let me tell you, if you come to the house of God, get on your knees, talk with the Lord. He'll fix you up! You won't need the Schick! You won't need anything else! You just need Jesus on your side. You can be victorious in His name!"

I'm glad this morning, I can stand on the Word of God! I'm glad this morning that Jesus, the mighty Lamb of God, died on the cross, for my sins and your sins, for the sins of the world. The Bible says, He was hanging there on the cross, blood running down from His hands and His feet! But He didn't say a mumbling word, but "Father, forgive them, for they know not what they do." Maybe you need to tell somebody, I forgive you for what you've done to me. Sometimes we get so stiff-necked, we get so stony-hearted, we don't want to tell anybody, "I've done you wrong, and I want you to forgive me." Let me tell you this morning, this is the preparation ground. You're going to have to get it right, right here on this earth, before you make it to the other side. Oh, Lord! I'm glad today! I'm trying to get ready, every second of the day.

You might say, "Brother Pastor, why do you preach so hard? Why do you go so hard?" I'm trying to make it in. I know works won't get me there, but the Bible says, "Work until the day is done. When night cometh, no man can work." When God has called your spirit home to be with Him, all your works are over. I tell you to work until the day is done. Put your hand in God's hand and He'll make everything alright. I'm glad this morning. I have the victory this morning, in the Lord, oh, bless His name today!

As I look around today, I can see I have the victory all over me! You might say this morning, "Why did Christ have to die?" He had to die to take away your sins, to take away my sins, to take away the sins of the world. He had to come like He did. But I'm glad! I'm glad today! I have a hope, oh, bless His name today! I have a hope in the Lord! I'm glad this morning. I'm glad He was hanging there on the cross, blood running down from His hands and His feet. But He didn't say a mumbling word, but, "Father, forgive them, for they know not what they do." He knew He was going to be victorious. He knew that God already had everything pre-planned for Him. All He had to do was keep His hand in God's hand. I want to tell you this morning, God loved each one of us so much that He sent His only begotten Son, and the Word says, "Whosoever believeth in Him shall not perish, but have everlasting life."

Let me tell you this morning, I see Jesus hanging there on the cross, blood running down from His hand and His feet. I see Jesus this morning. It seems like it was just yesterday, I saw them stretch Him wide. I saw them nail the nails in His hands. I can see them putting a crown of thorns on His head. I can see them piercing Him in His side. Oh, Lord! I thank You today, Jesus! Oh, Lord, I thank You for what You are doing! And then they took Him off that cross. They took Him all the way down off that cross. They placed Him in a borrowed tomb. Oh, Lord! The Word says, all day Saturday and all night Saturday night, He laid there - oh, bless His name today! Victory, we ought to have it today! I don't care what's going on, you ought to have a victory today. The Word says He laid there, all day Saturday, all night Saturday night, but Sunday morning, I can see the angels getting orders from God, saying, "Go down to the cave where my Son is. I want you to roll the stone away."

I see the angels coming all the way down, all the way to the earth, rolling the big old stone away, and my Jesus, lying there, oh, He was lying there. I see Him lying there, saying, "I've got to get up, I've got to get up! If I don't get up, they won't have the victory! If I don't get up, they won't have a way! If I don't get up, they won't be able to do the things they need to do." I'm glad He didn't stay there in that grave. The Word says He got up! I can see Him getting up! Oh, bless His name today! I can see Him getting up, taking off His grave clothes. I see Him stepping out, putting on an incorruptible body, putting on a body - oh, glory to God! - a body with no sin, I see Him putting on! I'm glad this morning! I'm glad today! He got up with all power! All power was in His hands! I'm glad this morning!

Somebody would say this morning, "I don't hear anybody preaching like that anymore," but that's what it's all about! Jesus getting up on Resurrection morning, getting up with all power, all power in His hands! That's what it's about, Church! Let me tell you this morning, if you're going to church and they aren't talking about the blood, they aren't talking about 'getting-up' morning for your Savior, I would say, get out of there. Because that's what God did, when He resurrected His Son! And one day we're going to get up with all power! I'm glad today! Thank You, Lord! I'm glad this morning! He got on that cloud! He went all the way, all the way back to glory! Oh, bless His name today! And He didn't leave me all by myself.

Somebody would say this morning, "Brother Pastor, you don't know what I'm going through. You don't know what I'm experiencing. You don't know what I'm dealing with. You don't know what they're saying about me. You don't know what they're doing to me." Let me tell you today, Jesus said, "I'm going to send you Something." Jesus said, "I'm going to send you Something, and don't you worry about them. Don't worry about what you don't have. Don't worry about how much money you don't have. Don't worry about your own condition. But I'm going to send you Something. I'm going to send you some power. Not white power, not black power, not any other kind of power, not the power of the atom bomb. But I'm going to send you power. Power, moving on the inside!" One of the prophets said, "It's like fire! shut up in my bones."

I don't know about you this morning, but I feel It moving inside this morning. It's like fire! Oh, bless His name today! I don't know about you, but that's the only way that a Christian is going to be victorious. He needs that power all on the inside.

Power! When they slander your name, you need that power. Power! When you're on your bed of affliction, you need that power. Power! When you can't see your way, you need that power. Power! When everybody's turned their back on you, you need that power. Your Savior has that power. My Savior has that power. That's the only way we're going to be victorious. Oh, bless His name today!

I don't know what you feel today. I feel this morning, I'm victorious in the Lord today! I feel like I'm seven feet tall! Not just in stature, but walking in the Spirit of the Lord. I don't know about you this morning, I just feel like I'm walking on a cloud. Oh, Lord! Oh, walking with the Lord this morning! You ought to walk with Him. Every day of your life, you ought to walk with Him. You ought to be able to talk with Him. I tell you this morning, I wake up in the morning with my eyes on Jesus. I wake up in the morning with my mind on Jesus. You ought to wake up with a song down in your heart. Regardless to what's going on, you ought to know you've got a song. I'm trying to quit here, Church, but let me tell you this morning, seems like the Spirit is leading me on a little bit further; but I'm trying to quit! Let me tell you this morning, you ought to have a song down in your heart. Maybe you don't know all of it. Maybe you don't know all of the chorus, but you ought to have a song down in your heart, that when times come up and things happen to you, you ought to be able to reach within, and say, "I've got a song, a song from Jesus, a love song."

I don't know about you this morning, but a couple of months ago, I got so in love with the Lord, I got some paper and I began to write a letter. I wrote a letter to the Lord. I wrote Him a letter, Church! Let me tell you, oh, you can't imagine what all I said. I told Him, "Lord," I said, "I love You, Lord! I love You in my heart. You brought me from a mighty long way. You filled me with the Holy Ghost and fire. You've been a Father for me!" Oh, bless His name today! "You've been all that I need, Lord. When I was incarcerated, Lord, You were right there with me." I don't know about you this morning. You ought to get Jesus down on the inside. It's the only way you're going to make it. Oh, bless His name today! I'm glad this morning! I'm glad today. Hallelujah. Hallelujah!

Let us pray at this time.

Our Father and our God, we've heard the Word today, for we are victorious only through You. And Father, we praise You today. We praise You for the ones that are here. We praise You, Lord God, for the message that You've given unto me. Not my will, but Thy will be done. Now, Lord, we pray that the message that You have used through me, Lord God, wouldn't go out on deaf ears, but it would go out and accomplish those things for which You intend it to accomplish. Oh, heavenly Father, I've been saying the whole month that the Word of God will either draw you in, or drive you away. And there are many, Lord God, that we have seen the power of God, the Word of God, drive away! Lord God, Your Word must be fulfilled. Bless us now with such blessings You know we are in need of. Thank You for the victory in Your name. Thank You, Lord God, for what You've done and are doing and going to do. In Jesus' name we pray. Amen, amen, amen.

CITIZENSHIP OF HEAVEN
Philippians 3:18-20

Gracious Father, we thank You now for this time You've given us. Lord God, as I would open my mouth today, Lord God, we ask that You would use me in a mighty way. Not my will, but Thy will be done. Oh, heavenly Father, we pray now that You would open up our blind eyes. Open up our deaf ears, Lord God, so we would not only be just a hearer, but a doer of Your word. And Father God, we pray now that You would give power to Your word. Wherever the word of God is going forth on this day, Lord God, give power to Your word, in the name of Jesus. And Lord God, we pray now for those who need a touch from You. Lord God, we are thankful for that song that says, "I was glad when they said unto me, Let us go into the house of the Lord." I was glad, Lord God, when they said unto me, and I'm thankful today that we can come in, Lord God, and we can leave better than we were when we came. Thank You, Lord Jesus, for what You've done and are doing and are going to do, in Your name. Thank You, Lord Jesus, for the miracles that are being manifested which only You can do. Thank You, Lord God, for being that great Physician, that great Lawyer that never lost a case. Now, Lord, we pray that You would move by Your Spirit in a mighty way, in the name of Jesus. Now, Lord, now, Lord, have Your way today, in Jesus' name, and we give You the glory right now, the glory is truly Yours, we give You the glory right now, in the name of Jesus, thank You, Lord God, for what You've done, and are doing, and are going to do. In Jesus name we pray, thank You, Lord, thank You, Lord, and thank You, Lord.

Turn to the book of Philippians this morning, the third chapter, and beginning at the 18th verse this morning, where it reads to us:

18. (For many walk, of whom I have told you often, and now tell you even weeping, that they are the enemies of the cross of Christ:
19. Whose end is destruction, whose God is their belly, and whose glory is in their shame, who mind earthly things.)

20. For our conversation is in heaven; from whence also we look for the Saviour, the Lord Jesus Christ:

A good Bible-believing Christian asked me the other day, "Reverend, if God is such a loving God, would He let a person die and go to hell and burn forever?" This person said he couldn't understand that. He couldn't understand how a loving, kind God who made all of this beauty that we are enjoying right here in Clark County today, could create a situation like that. Most of you know how I am. I told him, "I can't put you in heaven. And I can't put you in hell." But I told him of the story of Lazarus and the rich man. I told him, "There were two men. There was a rich man who had all of the things of this life; on this side, as far as earthly, or natural, this man had them." And I said that this man was going about his way, doing his own thing, as many of our friends and family members are doing today. And I said to him, "This rich man had everything. And there was another man that was not a rich man, but his name was Lazarus. This rich man saw no need in helping anyone." The story goes that Lazarus was poor and didn't have anything, and he would be content eating the scraps off this rich man's table. That was his only substance. Then one day, the rich man, after he had everything going for him, he built up more barns and had plenty, and his bank account was full, and one day he said to himself, "Now I've got it made. I'm going to sit back in my easy chair. I'm going to rest myself, and I'm going to enjoy the fruits of my labor." And the Scripture says there was a knock at midnight. That knock came, and it was the angel from God saying, "Now, tonight, your soul is required." Can you imagine some of our friends and families, if God knocked on their door? Maybe they're watching the sports, or maybe they're into fishing or hunting. If God came to the fish bank right now and called hundreds and thousands out here, right here behind us, on the river, and said, "Come on," what excuse do you think many of them would give? I can see them now, saying, "Lord, I'm not ready," or, "Lord, give me another chance," or "Let me run up the hill to that Baptist church where they can pray for me before You come." I want to let you know today, they won't have time.

I want to talk about this morning, "Citizenship in heaven." I want to ask you today, where do you plan on spending eternity? I'm mindful this morning that many of us are planning to make heaven our home. Many of us are making preparations even as we're here today, to meet the Lord. I want to tell you today, as I shared with someone this week, I said, "There will come a time when you will be looking for the Christians, and you will be looking for the church, and we will be gone." Folks will be coming to the buildings like this, and our building, and the buildings will be vacant.

Citizens of heaven are under a heavenly government. Other men are ruled by earthly influences of the law, of the state, of social customs, of worldly expectancies, but we, as Christians, are citizens of heaven. Somebody said that we are in the land of the living, getting ready for the land of the dying. I say, "oh, no!" to that. We see here people are dying every second of the day. Some of them are dying materially. Some of them are dying mentally. Some of them are dying because of being killed, and dope, and alcohol, and everything else. And some of us are killing our own selves. Some of us are killing one another. I'm mindful today, in the book of James, James said that there is a small member of the body, and that small member of the body is more deadly than a gun, or any kind of weapon that you can think of. He went on to say that small weapon, as small as it is, is deadly, and it's the tongue. We have to be careful, sisters and brothers, that if we're going to make heaven our home, we have to act like it. The true followers of Christ obey the higher laws and we serve an unseen King. It is our recognized aim to do God's will on earth as the angels do in heaven. Oh, you ought to be about your Father's business. You might say today, "I don't know what God wants me to do." I want to tell you today, it's in the Word. We each are called to do a job, and I don't know what your job is. Everybody is not called to preach. Everybody is not called to teach. Everybody is not called to do this, that and the other, but each one of us has a specific job to do for the Lord. Are you about your Father's business? Are you telling somebody, "What Jesus has done for me, He'll do the same for you." Are you letting your light shine everywhere you go? Oh, bless His name today! I believe that many of the ones in the world today are out there because we are not doing what we are supposed to be doing.

Citizens of heaven confess supreme alliance to a heavenly Lord. They perform heavenly functions. To be a loyal citizen of heaven means to share in the common municipal life. I want to tell you today, you ought to let nobody take your joy. I don't care what you're going through, I don't care what your family or what others are going through, nobody ought to take your joy. You ought to have a joy that the world didn't give -- oh, praise His name today,-- and the world can't take away. I'm glad about that today. Your conversation ought to be in heaven. You ought to set your affections on things above. It shouldn't be on this world. It shouldn't be on the things we can possess right here. I've never seen a funeral going down the street with a Brinks truck going behind it. You can't take anything with you. We brought nothing in, and we take nothing out. Only what we do for Christ will last.

Generally, we, citizens of heaven are to enjoy the heavenly privileges. Citizenship is a privilege. You're not serving God, hopefully, because of me, or because of some tradition, or because you're being forced to serve Him. You ought to be serving God because you feel it's your responsibility. I'm glad today. I'm glad I'm serving God because of that. Because if I felt I wasn't serving Him because of what I want, or God, and how He was dealing with me, I would be like so many others. I'd find other excuses for doing for the Lord. Our chief concern is to do our work on earth as best to promote the glory of heaven.

Citizenship in heaven today. Whatever you do, it ought to be to the glory of God. You might say, "But, Pastor, I can't do very much. I don't have much to do." But just a cup of water will make a difference. Just a smile or a hello or a handshake or a friendly hug or any kind of thing like that will make a difference. Someone said to me, a year or so ago, "You hug too much. You hug everybody." I said, "But it's something about that love that the world didn't give and the world can't take away." I've got to love everybody because the Word says, "How can you say that you love God, whom you've never seen, and you're right here with your brothers and sisters and you have no love for them?" The Word says you are a liar and no liar shall enter the kingdom of God.

Citizenship is a privilege. This was well understood in Paul's day when some men prided themselves in being born Romans, while others were willing to pay a great price to obtain the rights of Roman citizenship. Englishmen now proclaim protection and immunity from foreign extractions in all parts of the world, on the account of their nationality. So Christians have the same privileges of divine liberty. They have safety, they have honor, and the company of a heavenly citizenship. You ought to know today that you've been bought with a price. You ought to know today that Jesus, the Son of God, came down from heaven, on this earth, to pay the price for sinners, like you and me. You ought to know that today, that you're not a citizen of heaven just because of your name. But you're a citizen of heaven because of Jesus Christ. Oh, bless His name today. I feel something now. You ought to know that today.

The influence of this act, if it is to be true that Christians are citizens of heaven, then it must be most important. Yet many men who consider themselves Christians live any kind of way. Oh, I want to tell you today, others have taken the opposite course, forsaken the joys and duties of the world, treating the earth as a sort of Siberia, where they live like exiles, waiting only for the time of their departure. But I want to tell you today, you ought to walk like a Christian. It ought to be something about your testimony. Everywhere you go, you ought to look like somebody. Oh, I see Christians sometimes walking around, and I don't have anything against blue jeans, but blue jeans that the bottom is all out, and the knees are all out, and you see them looking just any kind of way. But you ought to look like somebody. If you say that you have a citizenship in heaven, and God is your Father and He's supplying your every need, then somebody else ought to know it. You ought to have a light that's shining, and not just hiding under a bushel. It ought to be a light that shines. It should lead to living worthy. It is a disgrace for any Englishman visiting a country to abandon that citizenship, but Christians belong to a higher kingdom than any earthly kingdom. I want to tell you today, we have been bought with a price. Christians are therefore to see to it that they do not disgrace their citizenship by following evil customs of the world, but abstain from the fleshly lusts, as strangers and pilgrims, as I Peter 2:11 says. Living in the world and enjoying its innocent fruits in doing their daily work, they are to keep themselves undefiled and to behave with purity and charity. Oh, you ought to walk like somebody. You ought to talk like somebody. This citizenship that we're talking about this morning should prevent

Christians from being disappointed at receiving adversity in their worship. I don't care what you're going through today. You ought to know and everybody else ought to know that you've been born again and bought with a price.

I'm mindful this morning of a dear sister this morning that was at one of the nursing homes. She had a bone disease. I'm a living witness that I would go to the nursing home just to be encouraged by her. You could walk in her room any day of the week, and she always had a smile on her face. I can remember during the time when she was winding down and God was slowly calling her home. Her voice, praise God, wasn't very loud. But whenever you got up to her, she would always say, "I love Jesus." I want to tell you today, it's something about loving Jesus, it ought to make a difference in every situation.

As I move on this morning, I was telling my wife, and I've been telling her for years, I said, "Honey, if any thing would ever happen to me where I wouldn't be able to take care of myself, I would want to be put into a nursing home." She said, "Oh, no, I don't want that. I don't feel that we want to do that." But I told her this, one thing about being put in one of those kind of places, maybe I couldn't get up and walk like I want to walk, Maybe I'd have to just lay there in the bed. And every time somebody would go by, if I could move one hand, maybe I could just wave at them and just say, "Jesus, He loves you."

I don't know about you today, you ought to know today that Jesus is in control. Let me tell you this morning that you ought to have a joy, oh bless God's holy name, oh, glory to God, that's not like any other joy. I want to tell you this morning, I love the Lord. He heard my cry. I'm trying to move on here, but it seems like I'm going a little too fast. Let me this morning tell you that nobody can do you like Jesus. Let me tell you this morning, your citizenship ought to be written up in heaven.

Somebody said a few years ago, "I got a new name." Glory to God! It's not like it's written on the birth certificate, but it's a new name, written down in glory! You ought to have a new name today, written down in glory, that no man can wipe out. You ought to have a name today, oh, glory to God, that's not like your own name. I'm mindful this morning, when they went to Jesus in today's Sunday School lesson, they asked Him, "Are you Jesus?" And Jesus said, "I'm Jesus of Nazareth." Oh, glory to God! You ought to have a name today! Not just the name that your mother and father gave you. You ought to have a name that every time God wants to get your attention, He can call you, and say, "Come on up a little bit higher." Let me tell you this morning, you ought to have a citizenship written down in glory. I'm glad, I'm glad this morning. I'm glad today! I'm glad for Jesus, He died! He died for me! And He died for you! I'm glad this morning! Nobody can do me like the Lord! Nobody, today! You ought to tell somebody everywhere you go, "I love the Lord! He heard my cry." You ought to tell somebody, "I know Jesus will make a way for you." You ought to tell somebody, "I know Jesus will be all that I need." I'm glad this morning, oh, glory to God! I've got a new name written down in glory.

As I move on here this morning, they are expected to rest one day. I'm thankful to God, I'm going to lay down, we're going to lay down these bodies. They're going back to the dust. But let me tell you, one of these days when the Lord comes, I'm glad, I'm glad! I said yesterday, when I was putting the light out there, if the Lord came at that moment, I would go on up into the clouds. I don't know about you today, but you ought to have a new name written down in glory. Seek the Lord God's face and turn from your wicked ways. Then God will hear your prayers. He will forgive your sins. He will heal our land. I believe today, if God's people would get in sincere prayer, we could stop abortions right now. I believe today, if God's people would get into prayer, we could stop this gang situation. I believe today, if God's people would get into prayer, we could stop marital breakups and whatnot. I believe today, if God's people would get into prayer, the jailhouses would be opened. I believe today, the mental wards would be empty. Let me tell you this morning, the reason why the world is in the state that it is in, it's not that it's the devil, because he's doing his own thing, but it's God's people. If we would get on one accord, I believe we could turn the situation around. When prayers go up -- I'm a witness today -- power comes down! I'm a prayer baby. I don't know about you. I'm not just doing it on my own, but somebody prayed for me. Somebody prayed for you. Somebody is praying for you right now. I'm glad! I'm glad! I've got a citizenship, a new name, written down in heaven. Oh, thank You, Lord.

So many people today don't want to hear that. They don't want to hear that one day I'm going to leave here. But let me tell you, you ought to have a new name, written down in glory. I'm glad today! I'm glad for Jesus, the mighty Lamb of God! I feel like preaching now! I'm glad this morning! Thank You, Lord, for what You're doing. Thank You, Jesus, for what You're going to do. I'm glad today. I'm glad! Oh, bless His name, for what the Lord is doing.

I don't know about you this morning, I can only speak for myself. Oh, bless His name! I can only speak for myself. I want to tell you today, you ought to have a new name, -- oh, bless His name! -- written down in glory. Oh, glory to God! We baptized last Sunday, and I can't speak for the candidates, but they ought to be rooted and grounded in the Word. Let me tell you today, the devil is busy, but look at Jesus, the mighty Lamb of God, hanging there, on that cross, blood running down from His feet and His hands. I'm glad, I'm glad! They stretched Him wide, oh, bless His name, they pierced Him in the side. Call on Him today! Oh, call on Him. As I close this morning, look at Jesus today. They took Him off that cross, oh, bless His name, oh, glory! They placed Him in a borrowed tomb. The Word says, all day Saturday, He laid there, oh, bless His name. He laid there all day Saturday, oh, bless His name, all night Saturday night. But early, early! Sunday morning, He got up! He got up with all power! All power was in His hands. You ought to have some get-up power. You ought to have some power, when the devil comes against you, you ought to be able to stand. I'm glad today, I've got some power. "Where is it coming from, Preacher? What kind of power do you have? Do you have electric power?" Oh, no, that's not what I'm talking about. I'm talking about the kind of power, when they lie on you, you can go with the Lord, the kind of power when you're sick in your body, you can go with the Lord. "What kind of power do you have, when you don't have any money, knowing God will make a way for you?" Let me tell you today, Holy Ghost power! Jesus said, "If I don't go, It won't come." I'm glad today, It came down. I'm glad Jesus went all the way back, but He sent me some power! Not white power, not black power, but Holy Ghost Power, Oh, bless His name! I'm glad this morning for the mighty Lamb of God! Do you have some power today?

As I close this morning, look at Jesus getting on that cloud, going all the way back, all the way to glory. If you're here this morning and you've got no power, maybe you've never accepted the Lord as your personal Savior, you can accept Him right now. Let me tell you, nobody can do you like Jesus. No wine store, no crack or cocaine. Nobody, not even your husband or your wife, nobody! can do you like the Lord. Oh, bless His name today. If you're here this morning, and you've never been baptized, you've never accepted the Lord as your personal Savior, you can come now, just as you are. You don't have to get yourself ready. Somebody said, on the other Sunday, "Wait until I quit smoking and quit lying." I said "NO! You'll never quit smoking, you'll never quit lying. But come as you are." Oh, glory to God. I'm glad today. I came to Jesus as I was, wounded, naked and tired. But I found in Him a resting place. And He has -- oh, bless His name -- made me glad. He has! Oh, bless His name today.

If you're here this morning and you're out of a church home, you've got no church home, and you feel the Lord wants you to be a part of this church family, you can come now and be a part of this church family. Somebody would say today, "Well, I'm out of a church, I don't have a home." Let me tell you this morning, Jesus said you have a home in Him. If you're here this morning and you haven't accepted the Lord as your personal Savior, you can come now. Come to Jesus.

GOD, IN SPITE OF
Isaiah 43:1-7

The question is asked this morning, "Is there a Word from the Lord?" I want to say today, there's always a Word from God. It may not come in the way that you think it should come. It may not come at the hour that you think it might come. But I'm mindful today, He may not come when you want Him, but He's always right on time. He's never late, He's never busy, but He's always there. When you need Him the most, when you think that you've run out, God just kind of sends a curve, like the Pistons did the other day, and won the game. Oh, bless His name today.

We're grateful to God today for what He has done, and for what He's going to do as we hear the Word. For the Bible says, "Faith cometh by hearing, and hearing by the Word of God." And it says, "How can you hear without the preacher?" and "How can they preach, unless they be sent?" We're grateful to God this morning for what He has done, for what He is doing, and for what He is going to do today. So I'm going to ask you this morning to turn in your Bibles with me this morning, if you would, to the book of Isaiah, the 43rd chapter. We have been in Isaiah in our Sunday School lesson all month long. We're just grateful to God this morning for His Word, for heaven and earth will pass away, but the Word of God will stand forever.

I said to a young man, "Happy Father's Day to you. Even though you're not a father, even though you don't have any kids of your own. It doesn't mean that you are the biological father of that child. It means being an example in someone's life in a fatherly image." I'm mindful today, I know some thirteen- and fourteen-year-old boys that have a baby. But that doesn't mean that they are fathers. I know some that are in the penitentiary, right now, that have babies, but that doesn't mean that they are fathers. I know some walking the streets right now that have babies, but that doesn't mean that they are fathers. I know many today that are molesting their kids. They have babies, but that doesn't mean that they are fathers. But we're grateful to God this morning that a father is someone who is an example to someone else, which doesn't necessarily mean that he has to be a part of that conception. So I thank and praise the Lord today, for this day, Father's Day. Every day ought to be Father's Day, but there's something about this day, which is special and set aside.

The 43rd chapter of Isaiah, and let us just read verses 1-7 together.

1. But now thus saith the LORD that created thee, O Jacob, and he that formed thee, O Israel, Fear not: for I have redeemed thee, I have called thee by thy name; thou art mine.

2. When thou passest through the waters, I will be with thee; and through the rivers, they shall not overflow thee: when thou walkest through the fire, thou shalt not be burned; neither shall the flame kindle upon thee.

3. For I am the LORD thy God, the Holy One of Israel, thy Saviour: I gave Egypt for thy ransom, Ethiopia and Seba for thee.

4. Since thou wast precious in my sight, thou hast been honourable, and I have loved thee: therefore will I give men for thee, and people for thy life.

5. Fear not: for I am with thee: I will bring thy seed from the east, and gather thee from the west;

6. I will say to the north, Give up; and to the south, Keep not back: bring my sons from far, and my daughters from the ends of the earth;

7. Even every one that is called by my name: for I have created him for my glory, I have formed him; yea, I have made him.

May God bless the reader and hearer of His holy Word. Thank you all so much. Let us pray at this time.

Our Father, we thank You now for Your Word today. Oh, heavenly Father, we pray that You would use these lips of clay, not my will, but Thy will be done. Oh, heavenly Father, we pray that You would open up our understanding today. Oh, heavenly Father, let us not be just hearers, but let us be doers of Your Word. Oh, heavenly Father, we praise You for those ones, Lord God that are celebrating this day, but Lord God, we pray that they would celebrate not the natural father, but celebrate the heavenly Father, the One who created the heavens and the earth, the One who spoke to man when he was clay, and he became a living soul; the One who took the rib of the man and formed the

woman in the image of God; the One that spoke to the light, and
where it was darkness, it became light; the One that spoke the
Spirit of God, and created, Lord God, this earth; the one that
sent His Son, who died for us, that gave His life that we may
have life, and life more abundantly, thank You for that Father,
today! Thank You, Lord God, for what You're going to do in the
service today. Let the Spirit of God go from beyond these walls
and go out into the neighborhood! Go out where sin is raging!
Go out where folks are complacent, and wake them up today! In
the name of Jesus! Now, we pray You'd have Your way. Give
free course to Your Word today, in Jesus' name we pray, amen,
amen and amen.

Again, we're thankful to God this morning, for the Word of God. I'm just mindful today of a mother who told me just a few months ago that her 12-year-old came in and she had told her not to be out late, but she came in late anyway. When she said something to her when she came in late, said the girl slapped her face, slapped the mother's face. The mother was disturbed, she was hurt, she felt this, that, and the other. I told the mother, "Society says that I'm supposed to love my mother and my father because they brought me in the world. But unless I demand that they love me, unless I tell them 'You're going to love me, regardless,' society will tell them, 'As long as you're doing for me, I love you, and when you no longer want to do for me, I don't want to have anything to do with you.'" Society says that. Society says, "As long as you're giving me, then I can give back. But when I can no longer get from you, then I don't want any part of you."

Many mothers today, and many fathers today, think that their kids are suppose to love them. But again, I say, you're supposed to force your kids to love you. I know my father and my mother told us, "You're going to love me anyhow, because I'm you're parent. I'm the one that brought you here." I know Dad used to say all the time, to some of us, "I'll put you in the grave. I brought you here, and I'll send you back." But what I'm saying this morning is that society is teaching a totally different set of concepts.

So, a lot of people today feel that because they're my kids, they're supposed to love me. But I'm grateful to God today, that love has to be taught. It has to be demanded, and unless we do it at home, society is not going to do it for us. It disturbs me when I hear parents who talk about, "Oh, they've taken prayer out of the school. Oh, they won't let my kids pray in school. Oh, they won't let them say grace over their food." And I say to those parents, "You can't expect the school system to teach something that you aren't teaching. You aren't praying with them. You aren't at their bedside at night when they go to bed, telling them to thank God for the day, and to thank God for the home. You aren't doing it, how can you expect the world to do it? The world is going to teach them just what the world is teaching everybody else." But I tell you today, you ought to be teaching them at home. You ought to tell them at home that you're going to serve God. You ought to tell them at home that you've got to respect not only your brothers and your sisters, but you've got to respect everybody! Oh, bless His name.

Let me move on here this morning. I feel like preaching today. I feel it today! I know it's the Spirit of God. Chapter 43, verse 2, where our text is coming from this morning:

"When thou passest through the waters, I will be with thee; and through the rivers, they shall not overflow thee: when thou walkest through the fire, thou shalt not be burned; neither shall the flame kindle upon thee."

I want to talk about this morning, the thought of the subject today, "God, In Spite Of." God, in spite of. In spite of all that's going on around you, it ought to be God, in spite of the difficulties. God, in spite of the sickness. God, in spite of the famine. God, in spite of the devastations. God, in spite of whatever it might be. It ought to be God, in spite of.

Judah is in Babylon. They are slaves there, for their sins. God permitted a wicked nation, Babylon, to take them from freedom to slavery; from a land they knew to a land they knew not; from a land He gave them to one He did not intend them to be in. They are slaves in Babylon, a strange land. The time comes for God to speak. After 70 years, He speaks to them.

Do you not know that God is speaking today? You might say this morning, "I don't hear any thunder. I don't hear any rolling wind. I don't hear any voices from heaven." But you do hear them. For the Word says when these things begin to happen, the time is nigh. When mothers are against daughters and fathers are against sons, when you begin to see famine in the land, and when you begin to hear about floods in Arkansas, where folks are being killed, and you begin to hear of people in Detroit that are rejoicing and seven or eight people killed, and twenty injured, and all kinds of things happening, the Word says the time is nigh. God is trying to get our attention. God is speaking to us through His Word. Are you listening to Him? Are you reading His Word?

After 70 years of slavery, pain, misery, and sorrow, God speaks. And do you not know that God is speaking right now? He's trying to get our attention in every way possible. But I believe today, there is going to come a time when God is going to begin to turn a deaf ear. God is going to begin to say, "I'm not going to hear you any more. I'm going to let you go on about your business, and do whatever it is that you want to do." I see that today. I see it happening in the churches, all over this country. Why do you think there's so much sickness in the church? Why do you think there's so much hell being raised in the church? Because God is saying, "I'm going to put my wrath and start my wrath at the household of God." It's going to start right here, at Everlasting. It's going to start at Bright Star, New Hope, Vancouver Avenue, wherever it is, it's going to start right there. But God is going to clean it out. He's cleaning it out every day. He's moving ones here, He's moving ones there, He's moving ones here, there and everywhere, so that He can use them to His glory.

I said to a young man on the other day, "You know what? I've been here at Everlasting more than 10 years." And I said, "It's something about being a part of this church that I love." It's not the building, but it's something about, I feel good inside! I feel good when I think about the name 'Everlasting.' I feel good when I go up and down the highways and the airways; I feel good about that! I told this brother, "There's something about knowing what you have." I feel good about being here. I feel good that God has put me here, and apparently, this is where God wants me to be! Until He gets ready, I'm going to be here until He says something else. So I'm grateful to God. You, too, should pray also:

"Lord, put me where You want me to be, and use me wherever it is, for Your service, not just on Sunday, but use me every second of the day. Use me, Lord, for Thy service, that I can be a witness and a testimony, in spite of the condition that I might be in."

God speaks. He tells Judah to fear not. In Isaiah 43:1, God calls for courage. In a strange land, a miserable land of slavery among godless masters, God tells His people to fear not. "You don't have to worry. I'm going to be there with you. You don't have to fret. I'm going to take care of your needs. You don't have to feel lonely because I'm going to be there with you. You don't have to feel motherless, because I will be a Mother for you. You don't have to feel fatherless, because I will be Father for you." Oh, I'm glad about that!

In spite of all that's going on, God says, "Fear not. In Babylon, in slavery, without a peace conference with the king, without money," God says, "for I have redeemed thee." God redeems Judah, just like He redeems us. Oh, I'm glad today, that I've got the Lord on my side. I'm glad today, that I've been washed in the blood of the Lamb. I'm glad this morning that I know Jesus for myself. Oh, it's not the testimony of someone else, but I've got a testimony that my God is a way-maker. I've got a testimony today, He's a mind fixer and a heart regulator. I've got a testimony today, that can't nobody do me like the Lord. I don't know about you this morning, but in spite of all that's happened in my life, my God is able. I say all the time, He's not a small god, but He's a big God and He's got all power in His hands. I don't know about you today, but I love the Lord, and I love Him because He's been good to me. And even if He hadn't been good, I'd love Him anyhow.

I'm mindful this morning of Brother Job. Brother Job was told by the Lord, "Where were you, Job, when I made the heavens and the earth?" And I don't know about you this morning, but Job's testimony was, "Though you slay me, Lord, yet will I serve you. Though you take away all that I have, I'm going to serve you anyhow. Though my body be decrepit with sores from my head all the way down to me feet, I'm going to serve you anywhere, anyway, Lord God." I don't know about you this morning, in spite of all that's going on, you ought to serve the Lord. You ought to put your hand in His hand, knowing that everything will be alright.

I'm glad this morning that God said, "Fear not, for I am with you. Fear not, for I will be with you, even to the end of the world." No sooner than God said it, it was done. Not money, but God's Word redeems today. Not the price of gold, but God's Word is what redeems today. I want to tell you this morning, whatever you need today, you can receive it from the Lord. I'm glad this morning, He's a way-maker. I'm glad this morning! He's a burden bearer. I'm glad this morning that there's nothing too hard for God.

Explaining to Judah, after their redemption, God says, "I have called you by your name. Thou art mine, and you have been bought with a price." I want to tell you this morning, that God knows every one of us. The Word says He's got every hair numbered on our heads. If you lose just one of those hairs, God knows which one it is, and how many you have left. I'm glad this morning that my God has all power in His hands. For God to deliver and return man from slavery, from doubt to faith, from confusion to peace, He speaks these words: "If you love Me, obey My commandments. If you love Me, put your hand in My hand. If you love Me, put all of your trust in Me."

He speaks that man return from things and men to Him. I'm glad this morning, that I don't have anything before the Lord. Put your hand in God's hands and everything will be all right. To know God this morning means giving yourself to Him, trusting and depending on His Word. I want to tell you this morning, He lifts us from the place of destruction to the lines of victory. I want to tell you this morning, the way to righteousness is a narrow way, but the way to destruction is a broad way. I want to tell you today, I want to be on that narrow way, walking with the Lord, going on home to be with Jesus, going on home -- oh, bless His name today! -- knowing that one day, I'm going to make it in -- oh, bless His name today! -- I'm going to lay down my hymnal and my Bible, and I'm going to go on to a better place.

I don't know about you this morning. In spite of what's going on today -- oh, I feel it now -- you ought to know the Lord is a way-maker. In spite of what's happening to your friends today, you ought to know the Lord! He bought you with a price. He put something down, all on the inside! I'm glad this morning! I can praise His name! I'm glad this morning! When

God lives on the inside, you become a testimony! Everywhere you go, everywhere you go, you tell somebody, "I know the Lord, in spite of my difficulties. I know the Lord, He's a way-maker." You shouldn't have to worry about it. He calls us to battle, and life is a warfare. Every day, there's something that comes up. Every second of the day, we're dealing with something. But I want to tell you this morning, can't nobody do you like the Lord. Nobody can do you like Jesus! I'm glad this morning!

To fear is to fail to know that we belong to the Lord. I tell people everywhere I go, if you have fear, it is a sin. You shouldn't have any fear, knowing that God, in spite of every situation, your God is in control. I'm glad this morning, the Lord being ours, and we are His, in spite of, He carries us and He sees us through. I'm glad this morning! When God calls, there is travel to do. When God calls you, there is a work to do. When God calls you out, He gives you something to do. Ahead of you, water, drowning waters of defeat, rivers of sorrow and rivers of destruction are on the road of this life. But I'm mindful this morning, when Moses was about to cross the Red Sea, he had Pharaoh behind him, the Red Sea in front of him. They couldn't go left, and they couldn't go right. I'm glad this morning, Brother Moses began to talk with the Lord. And let me tell you this morning, when you have a relationship, you don't have to beg and cry out to God. He knows your heart, He knows it already. And Moses began to talk with the Lord. The Lord said to Moses, "Look at me, Moses, what do you have in your hand?" I thank the Lord today! He always gives you just what you need! Moses said, "Lord, I've got a rod in my hand." God said, "Stretch forth that rod!" I'm glad this morning! Moses stretched forth the rod! He parted the Red Sea! They went across on dry land!

I'm glad today, whatever you need, God's already got it for you! You don't have to seek what the Lord has given you. You've got it already! I say, use what you've got, in spite of what the world may say! Use what you've got, in spite of what your family may say. Use what you've got, not to the glory of man, not to the glory of yourself, but to the glory of God, and He will make a way for you! He will turn your midnights into days! In spite of these, God says, "Thou art mine, you've been bought with a price! That price is My Son, the mighty Lamb of God! I love you so much that I sent My Son."

Because we are His, we will reach our goal. Rivers shall not drown us. Fires shall not overtake us. Oh, bless His name today! In the midst of life's battles, their souls are tried, if they should turn from God, but God shall be with us. I'm glad this morning! Somebody would say this morning, "In Clark County, is God with you today?" Oh, yes, He is! Oh, yes, He is! I'm glad! I'm glad about it! Somebody would say this morning, "Is there a God with you today?" He's with us! He's never lost a battle! He knows your name today. Who is He who is with you today? He said, "Fear not, in spite of." Whatever the day brings, fear not today. Whatever those pains of death or sorrow bring, fear not! Put your trust in God and He will make a way for you. Know that He will! He'll help you today! He promised us many things, but let me tell you today, fear not! Oh, fear not! In spite of whatever, oh, fear not!

Look at Jesus this morning, on the cross! Oh, glory to God! Death said, "What are you doing here?" I want to tell you this morning, He's giving life, oh, abundant life! He's giving life to all those who are believers in Him! I'm glad this morning, I can stand on the Word of God! Oh, Lord, oh, bless His name today! Somebody said a few months ago, "Reverend, you preach just like you were preaching to 10,000." But let me tell you today, the Word says, where two or three are gathered together in His name -- oh, bless His name today! -- He said, "I'll be in the midst of you." And He's in the midst of us right now. I say, in spite of whatever it is today, stand on the Word, the Word of God. Let nobody, nobody! Let nobody turn you around. Oh, put your hand today, in God's hands and everything will be alright.

I'm glad this morning! They hanged Him high on that cross, blood running down from His hands and His feet. But He didn't say a mumbling word! I'm glad this morning! I'm glad that He died there for my sins. He died for your sins. He died for the sins of the world. I'm glad! I'm glad He was hanging there. I'm glad! I'm glad the blood ran down from His feet and ran down from His hands. I'm glad! Oh, bless His name today! Thank You, Lord, for dying for me. Not man, not woman, but He died, oh, He died. He died that I might have life! I feel my help now! He died for us! Oh, bless His name today! Oh, bless His name, the name above every name! I'm glad He died there! But He stopped dying for one thief! He stopped dying to say to that thief, "Today you shall be with me in my Father's house." That's what I love about bedside confessions. I don't care how bad you might feel. I don't care what kind of liar you are. My God! Oh, He died for us. He died! Oh, He died for you, and He died for me. He's still dying on the cross. Oh, bless His name today! They hanged Him wide! They pierced Him in His side. Oh, bless His name today! And then, they took Him down off that tree. Oh, bless His name today! They took Him down. I'm so glad today! They took Him down! Oh, glory to God! They placed Him in a cold, dark tomb, all day, all day Saturday, all night, all night Saturday night. Oh, Lord! He laid there, oh, He laid there: all power, all power!

On Sunday morning, I can see the angels coming down all the way from heaven, and rolling the stone away. That big, old stone, they rolled away. My Savior! Oh, glory to God! I see Him now, I see Him now, taking off His grave clothes. Oh, bless His name! He said, "All power! All power is in my hands." I'm glad this morning! You ought to have some get-up power. You ought to have some power to give you life! You ought to have some power to make you live right. You ought to have some power to stand on His Word today!

I'm glad this morning, He went all the way back, He went all the way back to glory. All power, all power was in His hands. And the Bible says He got on that cloud, and He went all the way back to glory. I'm glad! I'm glad He went back! I'm glad, I'm glad! But my Bible tells me He sent Something! He said, "If I don't go, It won't come. If I don't go, you won't have any power. If I don't go, you can't walk right. If I don't go, you can't talk right. If I don't go, you can't live right." My Bible tells me, He got on that cloud, went all the way back to glory. He went back to His Father. He told the disciples, "I want you to wait on me. I want you to tarry, I want you to wait. I want you to go to Jerusalem. I want you to wait there. I'm going to send you, I'm going to send you Something. When they come against you, I'm going to send you Something. When they lie on you, I'm going to send you Something. When they slander your name, I'm going to send you Something. When they talk about you, I'm going to send you Something. When you're on your death bed, I'm going to send you Something. When you don't have no money, I'm going to send you Something." Oh, glory to God!

I tarried just a few years ago. And when I tarried, oh, bless His name! When I tarried, let me tell you what happened. I got on my knees, and I began to talk with the Lord. I began to tell Him all about what I needed. But let me tell you! I got up! Oh, praise His name! I looked at my hands, and they looked new. I looked at feet, and they looked new. I looked on the inside, and it was new, too. I'm glad today! Jesus sent the Holy Ghost. He sent It down, all the way! In spite of, He sent It down, oh, He sent It down for me! He gave me some power today. Some keeping power, when they lie about you. Some keeping power, when gossip about you. You ought to have some keeping power. When you don't have anything, you ought to have some keeping power. I'm glad today! I'm glad that He sent It down, all the way from heaven. If you want to receive It, you can receive It right now.

VALLEY FULL OF DITCHES
II Kings 3:16-18

Isn't it wonderful, one day we're going to be with Jesus? I'm not trying to hurry it, hear me today, but I just simply know that there's security there. There's hope there, with Jesus, somewhere around the throne of God. There isn't much hope here! But there sure is hope there. Oh, praise His name! I'm not rushing it! I'm just simply saying that it's going to be wonderful. Oh, bless His name! I'm going to see my grandmother there. Oh, bless His name! It's going to be wonderful to see Old Lady Florence. Oh, praise God. Most of you all have living spouses and families and whatnot, but when somebody has gone on, and you know where they are, you feel good about it. You feel good when someone you know has gone on to glory and you want to be there with them. Not that you want to go on and commit suicide, or hurry up, but you know that where they are, Jesus is! You can be there also! And I'm glad about that. Do you want to be with Jesus? Praise God! You need to give more than your right arm! You need to give your soul! And your mind! Your body won't get there, but your soul will be with Him! That body's going back to the dirt, to the dust! That soul, that Spirit within, that breath of life, that's what He wants! He doesn't want that body! That body's filled with corruption and sin! But your soul, that's what He wants.

Is there a Word from the Lord? There's always a Word from God. And it doesn't always come the way we want to hear it. But God always has a Word for His people. Second Kings, chapter 3, verses 16, 17, and 18:

> 16. And he said, Thus saith the LORD, Make this valley full of ditches.
> 17. For thus saith the LORD, Ye shall not see wind, neither shall ye see rain; yet that valley shall be filled with water, that ye may drink, both ye, and your cattle, and your beasts.
> 18. And this is but a light thing in the sight of the LORD: he will deliver the Moabites also into your hand.

May God bless the hearer and reader of His holy Word. I want to talk about, from the thought of the subject this morning, "Valley Full of Ditches." I felt led this morning to go that way, because I felt that we who are present this morning need to know that everybody is in some kind of ditch. It may not be a well, but there's a ditch that every one of us is in.

I'm mindful this morning that there was a man who had a donkey. This donkey was a real hard worker. This donkey had done a lot of service for his master. One day, the master left his home and he would normally ride or carry his donkey with him, but he decided to leave him at home. He left the animal at home and went on about his business. When he returned, he looked for his animal. The animal was nowhere in sight. He searched around the property and couldn't find him. He happened to hear a noise. That noise was coming from the old well. The man went over to the well, and there his donkey had fallen into the well. The man said, "Oh, God, my animal, the one that has been my trusted companion, is in the well." And you know how we are. We get frantic. He went and he tried everything to get this animal out. He lowered a rope. He lowered the buckets. Everything he thought about, and nothing he could think of could save his animal from the well.

So he thought to himself, "Well, he's been good to me. The least I can do is bury him in a good way, in the well." So he went and got his tractor, and he brought up all of this dirt and he put it beside the well. He got his shovel, and his animal was there in the bottom of the well, carrying on. He began to stick his shovel into the dirt, and toss big heaps of dirt right into the well, right on top of the donkey. Every time he would toss big shovels of dirt over on the donkey in the well, the donkey would shake it off his back, and stomp it under his feet. This went on, and it went on and on and on, and pretty soon, this man had heaped all of the dirt that he had into the well. When he looked around, the donkey was standing up on the well! Oh, bless the name of the Lord!

What I'm saying, my sisters and brothers, is that a lot of us are in a valley full of ditches. But that doesn't mean that you have to stay there! Because God has got a way out! Here this donkey was, every time the dirt would hit his back, he would shake it off, and he would stomp it underneath his feet.

The scripture in verses 16-18 says:

"And he said, Thus saith the Lord, Make this valley full of ditches. For thus saith the Lord, Ye shall not see wind, neither shall ye see rain: yet that valley shall be filled with water, that ye may drink, both ye, and your cattle, and your beasts. And this is but a light thing in the sight of the Lord: he will deliver the Moabites also into your hands."

The thing that makes God the most outstanding character in the universe is His ability to do unusual things. As we look around today, we can see that we've not had any major catastrophes in our area, but parts of Arkansas, parts of Louisiana, other parts of our country, have been devastated by floods, hurricanes, tornadoes, and the like. God is the only being in the universe that cannot be outdone. Whatever difficulty to be overcome in the world that cannot be accomplished is the place where God takes over. You might say this morning, "I've got some unsaved loved ones." That's a job for the Lord. You might say, "I know somebody that's on his bed of affliction." That's a job for the Lord, when the doctors have given him up. You might say, "I don't have any money! I don't know where I'm going to get my next meal." That's a job for the Lord. You might say, "I don't know, I don't know, I don't know, I don't know, I don't know!" That's a job for the Lord, for He takes the impossible things with man, and makes them possible with God. These truths are clearly demonstrated in the passage selected for the text at this time.

There was a struggle for power between the kings of the plains and the kings of Israel and Judah, which brought them to points at a place of disadvantage. At the end of seven days journey, they came to the border of Samaria, which was quite dry and arid. This condition imposed upon them a great problem, because they had great herds of cattle, camels and other animals, and thousands of soldiers that had to be cared for. Do you remember in Bible Studies, we studied about how Moses led the children all around Israel and all through the Promised Land, for forty years? And how through that forty years of travel, how God took and fed them, how God took and clothed them, how God supplied their every need?

Because of being confronted with such problems, Jehosaphat, the king of Judah, asked a question, which has been asked throughout the ages, in the times of great calamities, when mankind is confronted with problems too great for him to handle, so he said, "Is there not a prophet of the Lord, that we may inquire of the Lord by him?" I want to tell you this morning, you can have the greatest doctor in medical history. You can have the greatest attorney, F. Lee Bailey, or any other attorney. But let me tell you this morning, if you've got a prophet or preacher from God, it makes a difference. The preacher in a person's life makes a difference. It makes a difference in my own life. It makes a difference in your life, when you can go to someone who can not only give you the natural, but can give you the supernatural. He can tell you what thus saith the Lord, because it is the place of the prophet to keep mankind informed as to God's will and purpose of the future and the present.

Oh, I'm glad this morning, there is a Word from the Lord. You might say this morning, "Oh, I feel good now." You might say this morning, "Is there a Word from the Lord for me?" Let me tell you today, the Lord is trying to get all of our attention. He's trying to get our attention in so many ways.

One of the kings of Israel's servants answered and said, "Here is Elisha, the son of Shaphat, which poured water on the hands of Elijah." Elijah had been lifted into heaven on a chariot. You know the story. It says Elijah is the only one that went on up, and you never found a grave. Somebody would say this morning, did they find a grave for Moses? Oh, yes, they did. Did they find a grave for Abraham? Oh, yes, they did. But they said Elijah got on a chariot, a fiery chariot, and went on home to be with the Lord.

Oh, I'm glad this morning, that Jesus is coming back. And He's not coming back down to this earth, but He's coming in the clouds. I want to ask you this morning, will you meet Him in the clouds? Will you be ready to meet the Lord in the air? I'm glad this morning. If you're tangled up down here, you'll never meet Him up there. I want to tell you this morning, I know many Christians who say they love the Lord, but if Jesus came in the clouds in this very instant, they wouldn't go any higher than the rope that they're tangled up to. Let me tell you this morning, you've got to get up! The Word says, you've got to mount up on wings of eagles. You've got to mount up - oh, bless His name - and go on up to be with the Lord!

I'm glad this morning! I haven't arrived yet, but I'm trying every day to reach that perfection in the Lord. I had a man tell me yesterday who was confessing to be an atheist, he said to me, "I want you to preach a good sermon tomorrow." I want to tell you, God will make your enemies your footstools! Don't you worry about what ditch you may be in! Look at that animal. He was in a ditch. But look at God! The donkey shook it off his back, and he tromped it underneath his feet! And he came on up a little bit higher! Let me tell you this morning, when ones try to keep you in a ditch, don't you worry! Shake it off and tromp it underneath your feet! And let the Lord take control.

I'm glad this morning, as I move on here, Elisha followed Elijah closely enough to get his spirit. For Elijah said, "If you see me, Son, when I get caught up, I'm going to give you my spirit." Let me tell you this morning, I want the Spirit! I want the Spirit of Jesus! Jesus said, "If I don't go, It won't come!" Let me tell you this morning, you need to have the Spirit of the living God, the Spirit that'll make you love your enemies, the Spirit that will make you act right, the Spirit that'll make you do right, the Spirit! I'm glad this morning! I'm looking to the Lord today! Not my will, as Jesus said, but my Father's will ought to be done, not only on the earth, but in me! Do you want the Spirit of God working within you? Not just on Sundays, but every day of the week! I'm glad, I'm glad this morning! Oh, glory to God!

Elisha was in the crowd of three kings and throngs of people and animals who needed his word. Let me tell you this morning, God wants to use every one of us in a mighty way. Are you letting your light shine before men, women, boys and girls, glorifying your Father, which is in heaven? I'm glad today! Everywhere I go, I want to glorify, not myself, I want to glorify, not Everlasting Baptist Church, I want to glorify my heavenly Father, the One who saved me, the One who sent His Son down, the One who sent the Holy Ghost! I'm glad today! A valley full of ditches, don't worry about it! Just press on with the Lord! He has a way, a way out of no way! I'm glad today! I can call on His holy name! I feel it now, moving down on the inside! I want to tell you today, it's something about loving Jesus, my

Savior! It's something about loving the Lord with all your heart! It's something about -- oh, glory to God! -- I love Him today! I love You, Lord, with all my heart! I want to tell you today, I love Him today! Oh, bless His holy name!

Let me tell you today, Elisha was in the crowd, and they knew what they needed. There's one thing about being in the service of the Lord, somebody's watching you at all times. And remember, they are watching with critical eyes. Oh, bless His name! I remember when ones used to say what they thought. But my heart was in the right perspective. Let me tell you this morning, they can say what they want to say! You ought to know today, I've got Jesus, and I want the Lord's will in my life. Not anybody else's will, but Your will, Lord!

Elisha had been faithful as a servant to Elijah, to the extent that when the need of a prophet arose, the servant of the king said, "Elisha, the son of Shaphat, which poured water on the hands of Elijah, is here in the crowd." Let me tell you this morning, when you're a child of God, they'll point you out! When you're a child of God, there's a difference about you! I told a young man that was working on the carpet on yesterday, he was talking about going out to the night clubs on last night, and I told him, "Even if I went, they would probably put me out, because they would know that I have no business in there." There's something about being a child of God; you ought to walk different, you ought to talk different, your conversation ought to be different. I'm glad today! But the only way, you've got to be born again! You've got to be washed in the blood of the Lamb, Mary's Baby! I'm glad this morning, I can call on His name, the name of Jesus! There's power in His name!

The Word says they called Elisha, and because of him being of modest character, he somewhat strayed away, but finally went into action and began to communicate with heaven. One thing about it, when you begin to communicate with heaven, I can see, just like the jail cell began to rock. The Bible says that one night they had a prayer meeting, because their preacher was in jail. The prayer meeting was going on. The Word says Brother Peter was there in jail, and all of a sudden, the jail cells began to rock. The stone began to shake. Let me tell you this morning, when God's people begin to communicate with God, answers begin to happen. I'm glad this morning. They prayed and they prayed, and at midnight, oh, bless the name of the Lord, the jail cells flew open, and Brother Peter was led out of his incarceration, all the way to where they were praying. But let me tell you today, the Word says, when they heard a knock on the door, a little girl went to the door, and she looked out. She ran back, and she said, "You all are praying, and Brother Peter is at the door!" They said, "Oh, no, we're praying for Brother Peter, because he's in jail." Let me tell you this morning, it's something about answered prayer! You ought to pray and leave it with God! Leave your burdens with the Lord! Let Him work it out! And then, when they went back to the door, there was Brother Peter, standing there. God delivered him from the jail cell. Whatever it is, our God is able today!

Let me move on here this morning. Finally, the prophet went into action and communicated with heaven, and he said,

"Thus saith the Lord, make this valley full of ditches, for thus saith the Lord. You shall not see wind, and neither shall you see rain, yet they shall be filled with water."

Oh, glory to God!

"That ye may drink, not only just you, but ye, your cattle and your beasts. And this is but a light thing in the sight of the Lord. He will deliver the Moabites into your hand."

He will deliver joy in your heart! He will deliver peace in your mind! He will deliver healings in your body! He will deliver, whatever the situation is, God will deliver today! Just like He had done for them, more than 2000 years ago, He can do the same for you, in this hour, right now! Put your trust in the Lord, and He will make a way out of no way. He will turn your midnights into days.

This heartening message came directly from God through Elisha, the prophet, to the king and to the people. The Lord ordered them to make this valley full of ditches, and He would fill it with water, and with food, and with fresh air, and with everything that was needed for victory. I want to tell you, Everlasting, we're asking the Lord for everything, for victory in Clark County! Oh, bless His name today! I don't know about you, but I'm standing on the Word of God! Victory in Clark County! Victory, according to His Word today! Victory! Oh, bless His name today! I'm so glad, I have it already! I have the victory in His name, oh, in the name of Jesus! I have the victory today! Oh, let me move on here this morning! Times like these in which we live, to make these valleys full of ditches. Our valleys are not always full of physical ditches, but economic ditches, moral and mental ditches. But let me tell you this morning, you can stand on the Word of God! You can stand today, knowing the Lord will make a way out of no way!

Let me say this morning, I'm glad today, that God loved me. He loved me so much, that He gave His only begotten Son! Whosoever believeth in Him should not perish, but have everlasting life! Let me tell you this morning, you can stand on the Word of God! As I move on here today, don't worry about what others aren't doing, or what others are doing. You just keep your hands in God's hand, and everything will be alright! I'm glad this morning! I'm standing, not on the word of man, but I'm standing on the Word of God. Thank You, Jesus, oh, thank You, Lord! Thank You for the Word today! Thank You for the Word! Jesus said - oh, glory to God - "Man shall not live by bread alone, but every Word that proceedeth out of the mouth of God."

And I want to say this morning, will you go on with me? Oh, bless His name! I don't know about you this morning! Let's go on with the Lord! Be victorious in His name! Regardless to what they throw at you! Regardless to what ditch you might be in! Shake it off your back, and tromp it underneath your feet! Oh, glory! Oh, glory to His name! I'm glad about that! I'm glad about that! We can move on today, in the Lord's name! I say here, this morning, regardless to the valleys that you might be in, just let the Lord come on in and work it out for you. Let the Lord work it out for you, and He will, He will, He will!

Jesus died on the cross for all who have sinned and come short. We all have sinned and come short of the glory of God. But He died for us on Calvary's cross. If you're here this morning and you haven't accepted Him as your personal Savior, and all of a sudden you feel that God wants to do a work in your life, you can come now. I'm here to tell you this morning, Jesus is still doing great things. He's still giving sight to the blind.

He's still working miracles. He's still working miracles in this hour.

If you're here this morning, and you want us to pray for you, we want to pray with you. Somebody would say this morning, "You don't know what I'm going through, you don't know what's happening in my life," but God knows. Oh, bless His name. He knows what you're dealing with. I think too many times we tell too many other people what we're going through, and you ought be able to go to God. You ought to be able to go to your Savior, go to Jesus, and say, "Lord, You know what's happening. You know what's going on in my heart."

I'm mindful today, as we close this morning, we heard one of our Evangelists say last year that every time he saw a knight, he had on a breastplate, he had on a helmet, he had a sword, he had on everything that he needed to go into battle. But you never see a knight in armor with a back plate on him. What that says to me, is that God never intended for us to run from the devil. I want to tell you today, let's not run from the devil, because he's a liar. His time is running out, and that's why he's busy as he is. Let's keep our hands in God's hand.

Would you stand with me? Whatever ditch you might be in, whether it be a financial ditch, or whatever kind of ditch it might be, I want you to do just like that donkey did. He was going to be buried. But he felt something. Something about God, He moves in mighty ways. What I'd like you to do is, I want you to shake your shoulders with me like this. And I want you to tromp it under your feet. HALLELUJAH! Tromp it underneath your feet! Whatever ditch it is! Shake it off your back, and tromp it underneath your feet! Glory to God! Hallelujah! Hallelujah! Glory to God! Tromp some more, maybe you're not tromping enough! Glory to God! Thank You, Lord God. Thank You, Lord God.

About the Author

Pastor Willie F. Pride, Jr. is the founder of Everlasting Missionary Baptist Church in Vancouver, Washington, where he was the senior pastor for 30 years. The Lord has blessed him to baptize hundreds of people, many in the Columbia River. He has dedicated many babies to the Lord and he has performed hundreds of weddings and home-going services. He has been involved with a TV ministry that has been shown in Vancouver for nearly 20 years, as well as in Portland, Oregon, and five other cities in Washington State. He has been active in neighborhood evangelism, prison ministry, hospital ministry, and nursing home ministry. Everywhere he goes, Pastor Pride takes the opportunity to share the goodness of God with everyone he meets.

Pastor Pride is married to Dana Pride. They have one son living at home, three grown sons, four grown daughters, 26 grandchildren and 6 great-grandchildren.

<u>Books by Pastor Willie F. Pride, Jr.</u>

The Meat of the Word for Christians Today,
Volume 1
God Wants You to Do His Will

The Meat of the Word for Christians Today,
Volume 2
Everyone Needs Jesus

Volume 3 coming soon!

www.ingramcontent.com/pod-product-compliance
Lightning Source LLC
Chambersburg PA
CBHW061751020426
42331CB00006B/1429